HERREN'S
An Atlanta Landmark
Past, Present and Future

BY
Ed Negri

with
Michael J Cain

ROSWELL PUBLISHING COMPANY
2005

Roswell Publishing Co.
1005 Canyon Point Circle
Roswell, GA 30076

Library of Congress Control Number: 2004098867

ISBN 0-9763520-0-1

Manufactured in the United States of America

Edited by Phyllis Mueller
Designed by Ellen Glass

DEDICATION

*To Beautiful Jane
and my children Steve, Paul and Ellen*

ACKNOWLEDGEMENTS

*Thanks to Celestine Sibley,
who encouraged me to finish this book;
all my friends at Mt. Aire Realty in Ellijay, Georgia;
Tom Norman;
Elizabeth "Missy" Smith Aversa;
and Mike Cain and Bill & Peg Balzer,
without whom this book would never have seen print.*

*And of course, thank you to Beautiful Jane,
who has supported me through sixty-one happy years of marriage.*

CONTENTS

Introduction

As you set out for Ithaka
hope your road is a long one,
full of adventure, full of discovery.
Laistrygonians, Cyclops,
angry Poseidon — don't be afraid of them.

My journey began when I joined United Parcel Service as a part-time worker during my senior year of high school. After graduation I worked full-time and attended college at night, eventually dropping out. I promised myself I would return to college when I retired. After thirty-five years at UPS I retired in Atlanta. Within two weeks of retirement I was attending Georgia State University, fulfilling my personal promise to myself to finish my education, earning a B.S. degree in Interdisciplinary Studies.

In the meantime my wife Peg and I were introduced to Theatrical Outfit by our friends Graham Martin and his wife Joyce Bocher. Most of the work of Theatrical Outfit is produced and written by southern writers, with a southern theme, and provides a view into southern culture and heritage. Graham was president of the Theatrical Outfit Board of Directors at the time and he nominated Peg and me to the board.

Over the next few years I became involved with the day-to-day operations of Theatrical Outfit, and was elected to the post of Vice President.

In my role with Theatrical Outfit I came to know many prominent Atlantans. Occasionally, we gather our patrons for an evening of cocktails, food and entertainment. Tom Key, Executive Artistic

Director of Theatrical Outfit, explains Theatrical Outfit's mission. Under Tom Key's leadership, our patronage has expanded, and the work performed by the company has become more widely noticed.

One of my proudest moments, after being elected chairman, was speaking to these patrons at a recent meeting held at the Piedmont Driving Club. Afterwards, on the way home, cigar in hand, wind blowing through the open car windows, I felt honored to be associated with such a respected group.

At the third annual meeting of the patrons, someone suggested the group should have a name. One member suggested the name Ithaka, which coincided with the theme of being on a continuous journey. We decided that this well-regarded group of Theatrical Outfit patrons would be known as the Ithaka Group.

My personal journey continued as Peg and I decided to purchase the former Herren's Restaurant and donate it to Theatrical Outfit. This will allow the Outfit to have its own home for the first time.

The Atlanta Journal-Constitution covered the story of Peg and I buying the building that had been home to Herren's and noted the theatre would be a positive addition to downtown Atlanta. After the newspaper article hit the streets, I was contacted by Mike Cain, a writer and a friend from the days when our sons attended high school together. Mike was writing an article for *The Story* about how Ed Negri, owner of Herren's restaurant, voluntarily desegregated his restaurant in 1963 and helped guide the peaceful integration of all Atlanta restaurants. Mike was going to Ellijay the next day to interview Ed and asked if I would like to ride along.

That visit and many more led Peg, Mike and me to the idea of publishing Ed's memoirs. As Mike and I got closer to publication, Ed found information about the first blacks to be served at Herren's restaurant. They were Dr. and Mrs. Lee Shelton, and Mrs. Shelton's mother.

In August 2004, Ed found Dr. Shelton and shared an extended reminiscence with him. Peg and I were excited to hear that they had reconnected. Soon after, Peg and I met with Lee and Delores Shelton at their home. I explained our history with Theatrical Outfit, finding Ed and Jane, our involvement with the former Herren's restaurant, and the publishing of Ed's memoirs.

Dr. Shelton recalled his experiences of being unable to join many hospitals or doctors' societies because they were segregated. He told of Jessie Hill, Jr., the retired chairman & CEO of Atlanta Life Insurance Company, who was instrumental in organizing the community to work toward integration. I was curious whether Lee was afraid the day he walked into Herren's for dinner. "By 1963," he said, "everyone was beyond scared. One did what one had to do to fight for equality."

I look forward to reuniting the Sheltons and the Negris at the gala opening of the Balzer Theatre at Herren's in January 2005. Although it would appear we have come full circle, in reality the journey continues.

I'm happy to have had a hand in making this book available; it's a fair tribute to Ed and his contribution to the city of Atlanta.

Keep Ithaka always in your mind.
Arriving there is what you're destined for.
But don't hurry the journey at all.
Better if it lasts for years.

Bill Balzer
DECEMBER 2004

Ithaka, by C.P. Cavafy
Translated by Edmund Keeley & Philip Sherrard

HERREN'S
How I Got Here

When I started this thing, my intention was to note what I could remember of Herren's Restaurant, which, over its long life, has become something of an Atlanta landmark, at least to my family. For years one of the few "decent" eating places in downtown Atlanta, it was a mecca for many who had risen to the upper income levels. Today it would be a preferred locale for the power lunch.

In 1934, in the middle of the Great Depression, a red-headed prize fighter named Charlie Herren decided to go into the restaurant business. He started in a little hole in the wall near Five Points and then moved to 84 Luckie Street. To no one's surprise, he called his place Herren's Restaurant. In 1939 he sold a one-half interest to my father, Guido Negri.

Daddy and Charlie Herren arranged a deal whereby they would be partners for a year and then Daddy would buy the other half of the business. That's when my life took a different turn, though no one, least of all me, suspected it at the time. I was going to Boys' High School in Atlanta and courting beautiful Jane Fuller, daughter of equally beautiful Ruby Fuller, wife of Dr. James R. Fuller. I was really not very concerned about my future as long as it included Jane. The coming war was a long way off, and I was hoping to be accepted as a mechanical engineering student at Georgia Tech.

During that year, Mr. Herren spent most of his time at his new place, Herren's Evergreen Farm, which was a long way out in the country at Clairmont Road and the then-new Buford Highway. My brother Reynold and I were pressed into service addressing some mailing pieces for The Farm, a task we did in the tiny downstairs private dining room. Mr. Herren's nephew Bob Stanley, who was working for his uncle at the time, was assigned the responsibility of feeding us. My earliest recollection of Herren's good food was the super sandwiches Bob sent us as we worked.

For those who wonder, "whatever happened to Mr. Herren" — he was not successful at the farm, probably because in those days it was thought to be "too far out." He returned to town where he opened several businesses, one of which was on the corner just below us, and which he named Herren's, adding he was back "by popular request." That enterprise lasted only a few months, but in the years that followed it added to the continuing confusion. Another, called Herren's Evergreen Farm, was located on Peachtree Street at Third Street, where the Scandinavian House (formerly the Howell House) now stands. Still later, he retired to Florida where he owned and managed an apartment building. Both he and his wife died many years ago.

Bob Stanley and I remained friends over the years and through our careers, of which his has been most illustrious. He retired from the restaurant business and was working as a consultant in our industry when the great restaurant critic in the sky said he had done enough a few years ago.

Once Daddy became Herren's sole owner, he started making improvements. In those days there was no air conditioning (can you imagine that!) and he was aware that something had to be done to improve his guests' comfort in the summertime. The method in use at that time was to place large oscillating fans on tall pedestals at strategic spots around the dining room. Intending to improve on this system, he installed a machine he dubbed "the cyclone" in the back wall of the building. It took air out of the alley, passed it through a wet filter-like material and blew it with great force into the dining room. This system is still very effective in low humidity areas but turned out to be of very little to no use at all in Atlanta. When it was turned on, the fan was so powerful that the tablecloths would stand out on the downwind side and ashtrays would instantly give up their contents, being thereafter useless. One summer of that was enough.

As we entered 1941, Daddy went ahead with his expansion plan, which included Atlanta's first built-up refrigerated air conditioning system to be installed in a restaurant. The few restaurants offering this amenity had done so with package units, which were huge and noisy and installed right in the dining room. Our system had the machinery in the basement, and the air was brought to the dining room through a series of ducts. Any business with this innovation was quick to display a frosty looking sign on the front door with the word "Refrigerated." Our new system, installed by Carrier Atlanta, was a dream come true and highly appreciated by our ever-increasing lunch crowd. It was the last such installation in Atlanta before the war (WWII).

At the same time the dining room was expanded by taking in the back portion of two small stores next door. Included in the expansion was the entire basement space under those stores. Other improvements included upgrading the rest room facilities, the addition of a space with four intimate booths, and even an office, which was previously lacking. The basement expansion translated into employee dressing rooms, storerooms, and a huge walk-in refrigerator, along with the equipment room for our new air conditioning system. To pay for all these new amenities, the project also included some seventy-five seats in the newly added back dining room; these were quickly filled by the burgeoning lunch clientele.

Daddy had been the popular manager of the Piedmont Driving

Club for many years, and he was well known to Atlanta's business leaders. There were two major social clubs in town, the Capital City Club and the Atlanta Athletic Club, as well as some private executive dining rooms. More private clubs in downtown were yet to come. The newly expanded and more comfortable Herren's became the meeting place for Atlanta's movers and shakers along with those who liked to rub elbows with the greats.

All the action was downtown at night and Herren's was right in the middle of it all. At one time we even used the slogan, "Around the corner from everywhere," and, in Atlanta, it was the truth! In the evening downtown Atlanta was swarming with activity with five major theaters and all the nightclubs of those days. The Rialto Theater, right next door, showed all the best Columbia releases of the day and the Paramount and Loew's Grand had all the first run movies from those studios. The Fabulous Fox, not far away, was one of the world's most exciting theaters with its twinkling star ceiling, drifting clouds, Mighty Moeller organ and Arabian Nights decor. The Metropolitan Opera Company made use of this stupendous facility every spring. You could still park on the street and feel that you and your car were safe anywhere you could find a spot. Or you could make like a big shot, spend thirty-five cents and park in the Belle Isle Garage next to the Loew's Grand Theater.

As World War II started at the end of 1941, Guido and his wife, Amalia, began seeing ever increasing numbers of men in uniforms. Many of Herren's regulars would suddenly show up as high ranking military men. Our two railroad stations, the Union and the Terminal, were becoming busier by the day. The corner of Forsyth and Luckie Streets had so many pedestrians, cars, and trolley cars that it seemed to be the center of the universe.

I had entered Tech in the fall of 1940 in the Class of '44 and came within a whisker of making the Dean's List in my freshman year, thanks to my days at Boys' High. That's the school that produced Dean Rusk, Ivan Allen, my kid brother Reynold, my big brother Pete Negri, now a retired Marine Corps Colonel and a notable in our family, if not yours, and lots of other notables.

I was majoring in mechanical engineering and had never considered becoming involved with the restaurant, even though my summer jobs in '40 and '41 were at Herren's. Guido and Amalia, like President Roosevelt and so many others, seemed to be making out OK without my help. I had very little to do with the business except to show off Atlanta's most beautiful high school girl at an occasional dinner.

Daddy, taking the war in stride, quickly volunteered for any duty his government saw fit. He particularly pointed to his linguistic skills (he spoke five languages) and touted himself as being able to speak and understand "southern." As he awaited his call from Uncle Sam, he added some humor to his menu with phrases like "Remember Wake Island. Use less sugar and stir like hell," and he offered "Free French" fried potatoes in tribute to those Frenchmen who had escaped Hitler's net.

At Tech, we had entered an accelerated program of studies, eliminating summer vacations so four-year courses could be completed in three years. I was having a tough time with physics, calculus, chemistry, and dating when tragedy struck. In August of 1942, Daddy developed a bleeding ulcer, was taken to the hospital, and died unexpectedly a few days later at the tender age of fifty-six. The war around the world was going full force and business was booming.

Suddenly my mother, Amalia, with little restaurant experience, was left to run Herren's all by herself with the help of her even more inexperienced but devoted children, Rose and Reynold, plus daughter-in-law Reddi (Mrs. Pete) and my future mother-in-law, the now-widowed Ruby Fuller, all of whom willingly reported for duty. C.D. Lemming, a former Piedmont Driving Club accountant, dropped by to offer his services and he was hired on the spot as manager. Herren's managed to survive wartime shortages of help and food, rationing, price controls, and no shortage of sticky fingers.

By the time I arrived after the war, Mr. Lemming had moved on to other, better positions, but many years later he returned to the scene as my bookkeeper. He told me Daddy gave him the first job he ever had at the Piedmont Driving Club. I'm sad to say that, while he was working for me, he left Herren's early one afternoon because he "didn't feel too well," boarded a bus for home, sat down, and died of a developing heart attack. His business life began and ended with the Negri family. C.D. was a much loved and popular member of the staff.

With the war's end Mr. Lemming's position was filled by a series of managers who were employed to keep things going when everything was actually simmering down. Competition was rearing its head and all the displaced people in the "Forsyth Street foxholes" were returning to their peacetime jobs. I had returned from my stint in the Army Air Corps, which had ended as a flying instructor at a twin engine school in Marfa, Texas. I now had a family of one gorgeous wife and two rambunctious boys, Steve and Paul.

I was working at the restaurant and working on finishing my education, which had been interrupted in the middle of my senior year. I managed to struggle through and finally received my BSME diploma with the class of 1947. I was now out in the job market that had recently become overcrowded as wartime demands subsided and the market was flooded with millions of returnees. At the same time, the usual smooth flow of people entering the job market every year had been severely distorted. Many of the boys who had departed high school and college in '42 and '43 as fresh faced boys were suddenly home as adult family men, all looking for jobs.

I finally managed to find work with Delta Heating and Air Conditioning Company. My title, as I remember it, was Engineering Cadet, but my job was bottom man on the totem pole in the furnace and air conditioning business. It was a dirty job, crawling around among the cobwebs under old houses, putting together furnaces and duct work. I loved it!

A couple of months into this wonderful job, I received a fateful call from Mamma. Her latest manager was a recent graduate of Cornell with a marvelous background in hotel and restaurant management. That young man, Charles "Chuck" Satterthwaite, later became my brother-in-law and a highly admired and loved member of the family. She said that he needed help (though he didn't), and insisted I was needed. Against my best judgment, with no knowledge of the restaurant business, with no desire to become involved, and over Jane's strong objections, I returned to 84 Luckie Street. I have sweated over that last sentence because it makes no sense, but you had to know Mamma to know that she was the personification of the European matriarch and an extremely persuasive person. That's how a guy with a B.S. in Mechanical Engineering from Georgia Tech spent his entire forty-one-year business life in the restaurant business.

Guido

Guido was a remarkable man, but mostly unbeknownst to me. Much of what follows has come to me from others, mostly from family members, for I'm sad to report that I didn't know him nearly as well as I wish I had.

Guido Negri was born in 1886 in Trento, a town in Northern Italy. Historically an Italian province, this area was given to Austria by Napoleon and only came back to Italy after the Great War (now referred to as WWI). Both Italy and Austria tried unsuccessfully to conscript Guido during the Great War, when he was already a naturalized American citizen.

One thing you've got to know about Guido is that he had a great sense of humor. One family story relates an early demonstration of this. At the age of about fourteen, he left Trento and went to London where his older brother Mario was working in a large hotel. Since Guido spoke no English, Mario secured a job for him as a bootblack. (Those were the days when you could leave your shoes outside your hotel door upon retiring and find them there in the morning—amazing enough by itself—all freshly polished. With the condition of the streets in the waning days of the horse and buggy, this was a necessary and desirable service.) Daddy approached his job with fascination and a little quirkiness. In spite of the language barrier, he understood his job and did it well. The shoes were all brightly polished the next morning, but on one occasion none were matched up nor in their correct places. And on his next job . . .

Then there was the time he brought home two little billy goats, one black and one white, as pets for his "two little rascals." I don't remember what happened to those guys but we always had some kind of pets. I remember particularly the rabbits in the pen at the back of the yard.

I remember his statement as he went through Herren's with his spraying machine at closing time, trying to eliminate those pesky flies, "And now, let us spray." There were times when the last guests were *really* last; staying long after all others had departed. When it looked like they were set to spend the night, Daddy was known to warm up his singing voice and launch into song. First quietly from afar, then louder so that there could be no doubt that he would be heard. His favorite on these occasions was "Home Sweet Home." This usually resulted in the departure of his audience with profuse apologies for their unintentional delay.

He was known to have a little toddy from time to time and had set up a signal with Herren's bartender (we called him the "salad man" in those days, mixed drinks being illegal) at which point a drink would appear on the corner of the bar. Daddy called his special a Jackass. He used to say, "Three of these and I'll make a jackass of myself," though I'm not aware of any occasion when that happened.

As the Great War (WWI) cranked up, Daddy was working for the Hamburg-American Steamship Line, on ships plying the Atlantic from Hamburg, Germany, to New York. Mamma was living in Hamburg, though she returned to her hometown, Molare, Italy, so that her first son, Pietro Giovanni, would be born an Italian citizen, rather than a German. We have a picture, which might have come from that time, showing Daddy with a beard and standing beside a motorcycle.

As the war heated up, they stored all their belongings in Hamburg and moved to New York. Daddy left the steamship company and went to work for the Biltmore Hotel in New York City, while Mamma stayed at home in Hollis on Long Island to await the arrival of Rose Josephine, and later Edward John and Reynold James. After the war, Daddy returned to Hamburg to claim their belongings, but none were ever located.

At the conclusion of WWI, Guido was in charge of the restaurant department at the Biltmore. The U.S. Navy asked the hotel to provide someone who could take charge of the accommodations and food preparations for members of President Woodrow Wilson's party as they traveled to and from the peace conferences in Europe. Guido was assigned this task, which he gladly accepted, so he was loaned to the Navy for the duration. While the President and his party attended to the business at hand, Guido was allowed to be on leave. He did some traveling and returned to Trento, where he visited his family. Though his U.S. Navy duty was temporary, he traveled in the uniform of a Navy petty officer and was much admired by his family and friends. Daddy's scrapbook contains an invitation to the White House from President Wilson, who also endorsed a picture of the U.S.S. George Washington for Daddy. This memento also contains the signature of the then Assistant Secretary of the Navy, Franklin D. Roosevelt, though, I am told, he was not present on that trip.

Guido came to Atlanta in 1924 from the Biltmore Hotel in New York City to assist in the planning and construction of the Biltmore Hotel on West Peachtree. His was the task of helping design the food and beverage facilities, and ultimately to manage those for the new hotel. He brought his wife, his high-school-age son and daughter and two infants (my younger brother and me). His work at the hotel was time consuming, and family time was very limited. Soon after the hotel opened he was enticed away by the Piedmont Driving Club, then and now Atlanta's most prestigious social club. Here, his time was even less his own. When we left for school, he was frequently still sleeping, having worked late the night before. When he came home at night we were generally fast asleep. In the summer of 1933, Daddy sent his family (all except my brother Pete, who was a student at Georgia Tech) to visit relatives in Italy, where we lived for eleven months, mostly in Verona.

Those were happy days with Mamma, Rose and Reynold. We traveled, mostly around Northern Italy to Milan (home of Daddy's sister, Aunt Valeria), Venice, Genoa (home of Mamma's brother, Uncle Dino), and Nervi on the Italian Riviera where Daddy's look-alike brother, Uncle Mario, owned a hotel. Later we saw even more, traveling to Rome and Naples, at one point traveling with Daddy's other sister, Aunt Maria. We met all of our relatives, and Rose met her future husband, Lieutenant (ultimately Major) Reno Barsotti in Verona. Reynold and I had little-boy fun . . . we were ten and twelve years old.

Aunt Maria's husband, Uncle Arturo, was a wholesale cheese distributor in Northern Italy and we rode around the area with his two drivers, Feruccio and Antonio, learning some less-than-drawing-room Italian along the way. I never tried talking the language back home because I was never sure of what I had learned from those two guys. Mamma and Daddy never taught us Italian (it was their secret language) and after the trip they were never quite sure how much we understood. When we returned in 1934, big brother Pete was just graduating from Georgia Tech. We had missed a year of school, but what an experience!

Several years later, Daddy left the Piedmont Driving Club after many years of faithful service. His departure was sudden and an unfortunate product of the times. Benito Mussolini, a fiery newspaper editor, had come to power in Italy and had become a dictator with dreams of expansion. He had earned a reputation for getting the railroads running on time, improving roads, and building many public structures. Somewhere along the line, he noted many European powers had colonies in Africa and other parts of the world.

Mussolini had been building a credible war machine and had conscripted all available males. Young boys had to join the youth organization, the Balilla. He built an air force, sending General Italo Balbo across the Atlantic to visit the United States with a squadron of twin-hulled, twin-engine flying boats built by an Italian company, Savoia-Marchetti. This was quite a feat for its time! The squadron toured the U.S., landing on appropriate lakes. One place they visited was Lake Havasu City on the western edge of Arizona. That's noted on my map as the site of the old London Bridge, a tourist attraction on Lake Havasu. I believe one of the planes still remains there, possibly at the bottom of the lake.

Ethiopia had become an Italian protectorate in the late 1800s, and at some time in the 1930s became a point of some interest to other European powers. Mussolini's air force mounted an action there, with one group of bombers led by his son-in-law, Count Ciano, who later wrote a book about his experiences. In that book he described the bombs dropped on the villages in grandiose terms, saying that the bursting bombs looked like beautiful roses opening their petals. His book was roundly excoriated in the United States, and the whole Italian adventure was soundly and repeatedly denounced in the press and on the radio (no TV yet). Americans' anger grew. A product on the market at that time called Campana's Italian Balm that was highly advertised dropped the "Italian" from its name.

Guido was as appalled as other Americans and most other citizens of Italian descent. He had been very active in Italian-American groups in Atlanta. They were a small minority, and looked down on by many Southerners as inferior people. There were apparently those among the rulers of the Piedmont Driving Club who took exception to his background. He was summarily dismissed because of his Italian heritage with no consideration for the many improvements he had made during his many years there.

I remember that summer when he was home all day working on the side porch with his typewriter. Of course, without me
knowing what was going on, he was job hunting. Apparently,
one of his appeals was to Carling Dinkler, owner of the Ansley
Hotel in Atlanta, later called The Dinkler Plaza, who would have
been well-acquainted with him and his work. (Guido was frequently mentioned in *The Atlanta Journal* and *The Atlanta Constitution* in connection with his many civic activities.)

He was hired and sent to New Orleans. He spent two years at
the St. Charles Hotel, part of the Dinkler chain. His job was to study
the food service at that hotel and the food service elsewhere in New
Orleans, then considered by many to be the restaurant capitol of the
country. Ultimately, he was to upgrade his hotel's food department
and apply that upgraded technology throughout the chain.

Because of the impermanence of his situation, he elected
to leave his family at home, settling for occasional trips to Atlanta
and one visit to New Orleans by us. While there he became a
frequent subject of columns in the local papers. Many of those writ-
ings are in his scrapbook. His music was a standard at Kolb's
Restaurant, one of the places he liked to frequent. One column
relates a conversation between the columnist and the chef of
Dinkler's hotel; wherein the writer asked if Guido was an Italian
nobleman.

In 1939 he found what he considered to be his golden opportunity, the dream of every manager who works for someone else,
when he bought a 50% partnership in Herren's and a year later
bought out the original owner.

I don't mean to leave you with the impression that we never
saw him at home. We did. But though he was a man of many interests and certainly not uninterested in his family, we never played

ball or went fishing or swimming together. We (Reynold and I) were little American boys with our neighborhood friends and pals, and he was an Italian man who had pulled himself up by his bootstraps and knew only how to work. He encouraged my model airplane building and was proud of what I did, but he was not at Candler Field for the big Junior Birdmen National Flying Contest (rubber band models) or when I experienced the thrill of my very first flight in a Bird Biplane.

I did go with him very early one morning to the Capital City Club where he set up his easel and mixed his paints to continue work on a landscape he was doing of the club lake and grounds. I thought that was fun (Reynold went several times also, I believe) but I never asked him to teach me to paint. I wish I had, because he was quite good. He left behind many of his paintings depicting Atlanta scenes he knew and loved.

The family always had a big lunch together on Sunday. He generally cooked the meals while we were at church, and they were always exceptional. After I met Jane, she was frequently included in those family lunches. He was really taken with her, as she was with him. On many occasions when Beautiful Jane and I went to town to pick him up at the end of his busy day, he would take Jane's arm and waltz down the sidewalk while I locked up the restaurant. One afternoon as Jane and I were involved in a looooong telephone conversation, he came storming in the door to find me on our only phone. He had been trying to call me to come and get him, but he kept getting a busy signal. He was *very* angry . . . until I told him who was on the other end of the line. But I set out to tell you about him, not us.

During the early 1930s he served as Honorary Representative of the Italian Government in Atlanta without remuneration, of course; he even paid for his listing in the phone book as "Italian Consular Representative." The Italian Consul at the time, Cavalliere Bollati, had been transferred to New Orleans, I think. Guido's scrapbook contains many complimentary letters about his service.

During the Depression years he would get calls from wandering Italians in need of help. He would feed them and lend them money. Occasionally one of them would insist on leaving something for security or pay. Someone in the family probably still has a beautiful handmade lace tablecloth. And then there was the cello. Why the fellow left his cello, I don't know, but that's how Daddy got it. After seeing it sitting around for awhile, he decided that since he already played piano and violin, he might as well learn to play the cello. This led to his musical trio. Rose was an accomplished pianist, and I was a struggling (ultimately unsuccessful) violinist. Sunday afternoons were frequently rehearsal or concert days. Since Reynold did not play any instrument at the time (he is now quite good on the electric organ . . . even reads the music!) Daddy would tell people, "Reynold plays on the linoleum."

Guido loved good music and was the moving force behind the Atlanta Philharmonic Orchestra. Mr. Victor Kriegshaber, an Atlanta industrialist and music lover, was the financial backer and president of the organization, while Daddy did all the legwork, assembling musicians, finding venues for practice and performance, managing publicity, and even writing some of their music. His activities were noted in the papers and programs of the times, but to him the payoff of all that activity was THE MUSIC!

When the Metropolitan Opera was in Atlanta, he entertained many of the performers and musicians in our home. All of us enjoyed the fabulous meals he and Mamma prepared for them. He had what he (and we) thought was a fairly good voice, which he demonstrates for a couple of dubious opera singers in a family picture. I am told that in the early days of WSB he even sang on the radio! The scrapbook shows letters from many of the stars of those days and pictures of Lily Pons, Beniamino Gigli, Lawrence Tibbet and many others.

Guido wrote many lighthearted compositions. A family favorite was "Rosita," for his daughter. Another was called "I Want to be Happy Tonight." It was a drinking song, performed by the trio in one of his favorite New Orleans haunts when he was there. For the Piedmont Driving Club he wrote "The Debutantes Waltz" which was played there for many years at the annual presentation. He also wrote two operas, "Cleopatra" and "Crinoline Days," which he completely scored. Reynold still has these monumental works, kept in what Daddy liked to call The Casket.

Another of his interests was writing. He knew many writers on the Atlanta newspapers and frequently contributed columns on food, music, and other subjects of general interest. In his scrapbook Mamma preserved some of these columns along with several about him from a New Orleans paper. He had an astounding knowledge of astronomy and wrote short stories about trips to the moon and life on Mars. His most extensive writing project was his novel, *The Agnostic*, about Atlanta and its environs in the World War I era. It is still listed in the archives of the Atlanta Public Library. I've always believed that, with a little editing and an appropriate cover, it could become a modern bestseller.

With the outbreak of World War II, he quickly volunteered his services as an interpreter (he was fluent in five languages) but his scrapbook shows his offer was politely rejected. During the war, he dubbed Herren's basement dining room (The Mirror Room) "Atlanta's first bomb shelter" and reprinted his menus with the added aforementioned line, "Remember Wake Island . . . Use less sugar and stir like hell!"

Several humorous anecdotes from his Herren's days have survived. One that I remember involves a lapel pin. It was a molded replica of a wood screw and a golf ball. The back was a large disc inscribed "screwball." Daddy bought a stock of them and would confer them on his particularly good friends, thus making them members of his "screwball club."

At the same time he installed a small dinner bell on the column just inside Herren's front door. The bell was inscribed with the following words:

> That all softening
> O'er pow'ring knell,
> The tocsin of the soul—
> The dinner bell.
>
> —Byron

Anyone wearing the screwball pin entering the restaurant was supposed to ring the bell to announce his arrival and, invariably, receive extra care and attention.

During his few years at Herren's, he attracted a regular lunch group of building contractors, some of whom were on the portly side. They called themselves The Glutton Club and would tell Daddy, "Please seat us over a beam." Sometimes there would be only two or three to start with, and they would sit at any table available. Like as not more would straggle in, seating themselves on the corners or replacing earlier arrivals who had finished their meals. It was not unusual to see six or eight of them grouped around one table for four. They were all charter members of the screwball club!

During a national convention (I think it was the fun loving Shriners) one sweltering summer day, the restaurant was packed to the gills with people waiting on the sidewalk. Several convention-eers who were standing in line loudly declared that they were so hungry that they would eat in the middle of the street. You didn't say things like that around Daddy without getting some kind of reaction. He went to the basement where he found a table and four chairs. Despite the fact that the middle of Luckie Street contained trolley tracks surrounded with paving bricks, he placed the table and chairs right in the middle. One of his waitresses (now we call them servers or waitrons) joined in the fun and served the whole meal out there. (You may wonder what happened when a trolley arrived on the scene. Not to worry; the town was so crowded that trolleys could not run due to the fun and frivolity.)

One evening there appeared in our dining room a gentleman who claimed to be the biggest man in the USA. (Those who were there agreed this was certainly possible.) He ordered a prodigious amount of food—two of this, two of that, and ended up ordering a whole apple pie for dessert. Naturally, he attracted Daddy's attention. When the man was part of the way through the apple pie he remarked, "This is so good, I believe I could eat another whole pie." Well, Daddy was intrigued. He then and there issued a challenge, "If you can eat another whole apple pie, I'll cancel the entire check." Well . . . he did . . . and he did!

Reynold tells me that when he was sixteen and a newly licensed driver, he went on a car trip with Daddy and Mamma. They went to Asheville, North Carolina, through the mountains on the roads of those days. Daddy was enthralled with the scenery, exclaiming, "Look at that!" and other admiring statements as the scenery unfolded. Finally, when Reynold's nerves began to get the better of his good judgment, he suggested that Daddy could admire the scenery to his heart's content if he would let Reynold drive. By Reynold's account, "He stopped the car, climbed in the back seat, let me drive, and never again drove with me in the car!"

Daddy was a gentleman and a scholar. He was also, at times, a nut. In August of 1942 he was suddenly gone at fifty-six after a brief stay in the hospital. I had turned twenty-one just two days before. I hope he has followed my career with some degree of acceptance or maybe even a little pride. And I hope that the ignominious end didn't disappoint him too much.

Amalia

Having told you something about Guido, I would feel remiss in not including some words about his wife. Her friends all called her Amalia, which always seemed strange to me as I was growing up, because we called her Mamma. Presuming that I will not write anything to dissuade you from considering her as a lovable friend, I shall call her Amalia here. Amalia was born on March 21, 1891 and grew up in the small Northern Italian town of Molare in the Alessandria province near Milan. At this writing I am unable to find Molare on a recent map of Italy issued by the American Automobile Association. But I was there when I was twelve and my sister Rose was there recently, so I can assure you that it really exists and is a charming little mountain town.

Family legend has it that she was descended from the del Caretto family, the local nobility. Also there is some distant connection with the line of Admiral Andrea Doria. We've never tried to prove any of this but it sounds good so let's leave it at that. I'll tell you what little I know, starting with the meeting with Guido.

On the Italian Riviera, just south of Genoa, there is a romantic village called Portofino. In the early part of this century there was a grand hotel, Portofino Kulm, on a mountain overlooking the little village and with a spectacular view of the Italian Riviera. The only way to reach it then, as in 1933 when I was there, was by boat. Guido and his brother Mario were working at the Portofino Kulm as waiters when there arrived on the scene Italy's very first female telegraph operator, Amalia Gilardi. Smitten with her dark hair and eyes, Guido serenaded her with songs beneath her balcony. His favorite, so I am told, was "Mia Bella Napoli." (Presumably, because of her flashing dark eyes, he thought of her as a Neapolitan.) My information comes in part from my younger brother Reynold, who shared her house for many years, and from Beautiful Jane, who cared for her in our home after Mamma's first stroke.

I wanted to tell you about this beginning because it points to her pioneering spirit and her willingness to take on any task. We next see Amalia in Hamburg, Germany, where the young couple lived while Guido plied his trade in the food service department of the Hamburg-American Steamship Line, traveling between Hamburg and New York. As far as I know, she only left Hamburg twice during those years. Once she returned to Molare so my brother Pete would be born an Italian citizen. The second time she traveled to the United States.

When Guido was transferred to Atlanta in 1924, Amalia brought her brood of four south. In those days, people with Italian accents were regarded cautiously and her efforts to join such things as the PTA were met with rejection. Despite this early discrimination, Amalia made many friends during her long lifetime in Atlanta. She enjoyed entertaining and was forever feeding strangers, from wandering Italian down-and-outers in the '30s to members of the Metropolitan Opera, from her own kids and grandchildren to her many friends. She was eternally optimistic and sometimes quite naive.

Though she never learned to drive, she owned two cars with Reynold as the only driver, and she would tell me things like, "The Bucket Six is the quietest car on the road." When I would ask her how she knew, she would tell me that she heard it on TV.

Reynold, always interested in things electronic, was eager to have one of the new-fangled TV sets. Mamma, the old-world lady, was adamantly opposed to the whole idea. So he bought one of the finest sets of the day and installed it in the small library of their home where he could watch without disturbing her. At first she would not even come into the room when he was watching, but gradually she would sneak a peek. When she decided to sit down and watch, the set was moved to the living room and it wasn't too long before she was selecting the programs!

One of her cars was a Buick convertible, which I loved to borrow. When I did, it was my duty to pick her up for the ride to town. One beautiful spring morning, driving with the top down, we were stopped by the police. "What's the problem?" I asked innocently as she started to dig in her purse. "You didn't come to a full stop before you turned right at the last corner, sir," was the respectful reply. As I went into my best apology, Mamma pushed a twenty-dollar bill under my nose saying, "Here, pay him and let's get on to town." Evidently sensing that I had problems enough, the officer advised me to be more careful in the future and let us go.

One of my earliest memories is of her final (and maybe first) driving lesson. Guido had bought a Nash, probably a 1925 or '26 model. It was a big box with the tires mounted on solid steel discs. The lesson ended around the corner from our Fifth Street house at the corner of Techwood Drive and Sixth Street when she missed the turn and broke off a fire hydrant. She never again attempted to learn to drive.

Whenever his lawyer suggested that a will was in order, Daddy would not contemplate leaving and didn't want to talk about it . . . he was still young and had plenty of time! When he died suddenly in 1942 at the age of fifty-six, he did so in true European fashion, intestate. Amalia was thrust into the position of major owner and operator of Herren's, with her four children as minority stockholders by order of the court.

She had worked with Guido for a few months during his short tenure; her main experience was as a mother and housewife. Now she was the 60% owner of this thriving business. With the aid of Reynold, Rose, daughter-in-law Reddi (Pete's wife), my mother-in-law Ruby Fuller, and C.D. Lemming—all of whom were willing but untrained—she kept the business running during the war years.

There was a time when Amalia would act as cashier and many of our public would see her making change while wearing white cotton gloves, of which she had innumerable pairs, because money is indeed dirty. You don't hear the term "filthy lucre" much anymore. Though many thought she wore gloves to keep her hands clean, the fact of the matter was that she had developed a bothersome rash on her hands. After trying all sorts of home remedies, she sought medical counsel. After much testing, it was determined she was allergic to silver, and the doctor advised her to wear gloves! Imagine her consternation in finding that, of all things, she was allergic to money!

I knew Amalia always as a person of moderation, and seldom saw her smoke. When she did, she would take a cigarette from someone and hold it tentatively between her thumb and forefinger, taking small puffs that she never inhaled. I am of the impression that she would indulge in this habit on the order of once a week and then one cigarette only. On the rare occasions when I witnessed this action she would volunteer, "I've got to give up this habit."

While she was a thoroughly Italian lady, I was a thoroughly American boy. During my times in the dining room it was my greatest pleasure to befriend and be befriended by many businessmen to the point of being on a first-name basis with them. The easy joking and insults back and forth among Americans rubbed her European sense of propriety the wrong way. One day, after she had overheard me greet one of my friends with, "Hello, you old SOB," or some such, she volunteered that I should not be so insulting. "You're going to disgust (which she pronounced *diz-gust)* the customers," she told me, "and they won't come back."

When I joined Herren's after my return from WWII, she was the boss of this now slowing business. The soldiers had gone home and competition was beginning to rear its head. There were more than enough problems to go around. I knew nothing about the business, but was willing to undergo on-the-job training from her, from my brother-in-law, from our employees, from all the salespeople who called on us in those days, and from various seminars and meetings put on by the local and national restaurant associations. As the years went by, she took more of a back seat in the business, ultimately selling her controlling interest to me.

In the late '50s, the business had grown to the point that we needed to expand. Through our accountants, Harris, Kerr, Forster and Company, we engaged a consultant, Victor Colucci, to show the way. He wrote a wonderful report on our business, giving us advice on why, what, and how to expand. Loosely following his directions, in conjunction with our landlord, and with Mamma personally financing a huge amount of the quarter-million-dollar expense, the restaurant grew to its ultimate size. The early '60s brought the civil rights movement to Atlanta with me as leader of the company and involved in many community activities, including the restaurant association

I'm sure that all who were present at this next-told occasion remember it as a highlight of the moment. A friend had just opened a new and very elegant restaurant called the Chateau Fleur de Lis. It was rightfully the talk of the town at that time and, as restaurateurs, it seemed appropriate to see for ourselves. Mamma invited Jane and me and our three kids to join her and my brother Reynold for dinner at this estimable restaurant. We were all led to our table where the captain, in the broadest possible French accent, indicated that, "Madame will sit here, Monsieur will sit here . . . " and proffered the enormous and intimidating menu to each of us. It was written entirely in French and unintelligible to everyone but her. Like most Europeans she spoke several languages, French being one of them. She interpreted for all of us and we told her what we wanted. When the captain returned to take our order, she proceeded to order in French, only to be stopped abruptly by the captain (he of the French accent) who said, in a very broad Brooklynese accent, "I'm sorry, Ma'am, but I don't speak French." She immediately retorted while wagging her finger at him, "Shame on you," and placed our order in English, following which he returned to the accent and said, "Thank you, Madame."

Amalia was still putting in a few hours a day at Herren's taking care of the bank deposits and such books as we maintained in the house. I attended what I believe was over 100 hours of meetings with other restaurant owners without her knowledge.

When a plan was worked out with leaders of the black community, I called a meeting in my office. Mamma was there, of course, along with several assistant managers. I told them that it had been decided that on that day (it didn't actually happen as planned, but several days later) we would serve our first black guests.

I told them I would call a meeting of our staff to inform them, telling them that any who wanted could leave without prejudice (none did), but all who stayed would be expected to give their wholehearted cooperation.

Mamma . . . Amalia . . . Italy's first female telegraph operator . . . the lady who had accepted the sudden burden of the entire business in 1942 . . . she who had previously had no knowledge of any of the goings-on . . . made a comment I have never been able to verbalize without a catch in my breath. She said simply, "What took you so long?" And I caught my breath when I wrote that twenty-five years later!

Amalia spent the last night of her life at Herren's with all of her closest friends. At that time we had converted our lower dining room into Herren's Gallery, where we displayed works of local artists. We used the room for dinner business on Friday and Saturday nights and had a pianist to entertain our guests. On her last Friday night, Mamma sat down on the piano bench with the pianist, who accompanied her as she sang some of her favorite Italian songs. The next morning she suffered her second stroke and, at seventy-six, was suddenly gone.

Restaurant Row

Established in 1934, Herren's was located at 84 Luckie Street in downtown Atlanta. In the '40s and '50s, the street name could have been "Restaurant Row" because there were restaurants everywhere you looked. Downtown was lucky to have us all in one spot. If you couldn't get a seat in one restaurant, you could easily move to another. One might imagine that from time to time each of us got the other's overflow.

Luckie Street always seemed to be an east-west street to me until they demolished the Forsyth Building across the street from us. For all my downtown days, this ten-story building housed an indoor parking garage with its entrance across from our front door. In addition to a few shops on the street level, it also had a few floors of offices housing some of our guests, including a prominent architect and all those wonderful people from radio station WGST. Demolition revealed the huge concrete proscenium arch of the old Forsyth Theater, buried in that building where we had always heard it was. Demolition of the Dinkler Hotel, on the other side of the Forsyth Building, had earlier revealed an advertisement for the Forsyth Theater on that side.

But I started to tell you about the direction of our street, which still colors my thinking of the area. As I said, I thought our street headed due west. Early one morning, after the Forsyth Building was gone, I was sitting in our back dining room when I realized that the sun was shining in my eyes. Since I was facing north, how could the rising sun be in my eyes? Had something changed? A city map showed that our street proceeded in a northwest direction from Peachtree Street and my compass proved the point. I'm going to keep referring to my old system of thinking and hope that the following words about the location of things in our area does not become too confusing.

Guido sloganed us "The restaurant of the Elite," because of his following from the Piedmont Driving Club. In later days we eschewed the word "elite" partly because it had become old fashioned and somewhat humorous, and partly because a radio comedy personality answered his barroom phone, "Where the Elite meet to eat." At a later time we used the slogan, "Around the corner from everywhere in Atlanta," which was reasonably true at that stage of Atlanta's development. We were just three blocks from Atlanta's famous Five Points, the center of the south and considered by many as the center of Atlanta's business district. Nearby were our two newspapers, *The Atlanta Constitution* and *The Atlanta Journal*, about a block each from Five Points. When they were combined under one ownership in a new building, they were and are still only two blocks from Five Points and, incidentally, just three from Herren's. When we had a third paper, *The Georgian* (a Hearst paper), it, too, was only about three blocks from the center. At one time, Woodrow Wilson practiced law nearby and all of the famous people of those days were daily sights on our streets.

Shopping in Atlanta was anchored by Rich's (you could take anything back to Rich's, even if you didn't buy it there) four blocks south of us and Davison's (owned by Macy's) three short blocks north. When Rich's built its store for homes across Forsyth Street from the old store, they joined the two with a tunnel under Forsyth Street and a multi-storied bridge over that street. When asked by a lady boarding a bus at Davison's, "Does this bus go near Rich's?" the operator is reported to have said, "Lady, we go over, under, around and through Rich's! Hop aboard." These two grand department stores shared Forsyth (accent on the "y") Street as a walking connector, back when people shopped downtown and thought nothing of walking. North of the one and south of the other were the great jumping off places. In between there were five first-run movie theaters, drug stores, restaurants, jewelers, shoe shops, and merchants of every description.

Recently, I was doodling on a pad and tried to name all the businesses I could remember that were in this corridor but were now gone. My total was about ninety and later thinking indicated that I had missed many. I wasn't able even to guess at how many offices had moved from our vicinity.

Our location was just one door west of Forsyth and only one block separated us from Peachtree Street where Luckie began. In only one mile, at the edge of the Georgia Tech campus, the name changed to Hemphill. A well-known business on this portion of the street was the controversial Pickrick Restaurant, our polar opposite during the integration days of the '60s. A mile further the name changed to Northside Drive, which in its northern reaches led to the mansions of many of Atlanta's leaders, including Atlanta's great and courageous Mayor Ivan Allen.

On the corner, next to us, was the Rialto Theater, a first-run house showing all the first-run Columbia Pictures. Diagonally across from it was the Piedmont Hotel, built in 1903, with a fine dining room known far and wide during the early part of the century. On a small corner of that property there had been a restaurant site occupied by a Krystal, succeeded by Johnny Reb's, followed by The Sportsman.

Across Forsyth Street from the Piedmont, practically in our front yard, was the Ansley Hotel. Later renamed The Dinkler Plaza, it was home to the Rathskeller, Owl Room (complete with blinking-eyed owls on top of the columns), and Starlight Roof, where Hollywood stars performed in a theater in the round. I remember attending a performance and noted Cesar Romero lighting a cigarette with a Herren's match. Many of the stars dined regularly at Herren's and I fell in love with Marcia Hunt! (Just kidding, Jane.)

The southeast corner of Luckie/Forsyth once housed the Melba Cafeteria, which became the La Louisianne Restaurant, then an oriental restaurant, and finally Leb's with its downstairs night-club, Pigalley . . . that's the way they spelled it. Leb's was downtown Atlanta's first big-time delicatessen style restaurant and possibly one of the best of its kind in the country. Farther down that block to the south of our intersection on Forsyth Street there were a number of smaller eating places, the most notable of which was Venables, widely known for its friendly owner, its wooden counter, and scrumptious country vegetables.

Around the corner from them and upstairs was The Ellen Rice Tea Room, which later moved up on Forsyth Street on the other side of the Dinkler Hotel next to the Carnegie Library and was called Dave Rice's, still only a block from us. To our west, Luckie Street was almost entirely composed of restaurants, the first one being Harry's Steak House right next to us. On the corner below, just across Fairlie Street was originally Harvey's (not the one of rail-road fame), which later housed another Herren's (Charlie sold out to Guido but just couldn't stay out of the business), then the Belmont Steak House, and ultimately a high-rise parking deck. The neighbor of this building housed the Davis Brothers Restaurant with its Tubby's Attic, named after S.R. "Tubby" Davis, one of the brothers. Also in the block was an early version of Howard Johnson's, later followed by a Chinese restaurant.

On the other side of the street in that block, the corner building belonged to the Ship Ahoy, which opened its doors the same year we did, in 1934. It later became the Knight's Table, which was ultimately torn down and converted to a parking lot. Farther down the block were a number of small places, one called The Old South that became Venables when that establishment's building on Forsyth was demolished. A block farther down was the Brown Derby, and even farther out were a number of small counter-type cafes. South on Fairlie Street, just behind Herren's, was Emile's French Café and its neighbor, Margaret's Tray Shop, a highly popular lunchtime eatery.

According to information I received from some source, now unknown, our building once housed the Atlanta home of Columbia Pictures and was the scene of a disastrous fire with some loss of life. The city quickly enacted an ordinance prohibiting the cutting of film (then the highly inflammable celluloid) above the ground floor. You can still see the change of bricks on the front of the building, and we found further internal evidence of this during our 1961–1962 remodeling.

During WWII, the offices in downtown Atlanta were dubbed "Forsyth Street foxholes" by Atlanta columnist Ernie Rogers, who mentioned Herren's frequently. He called us "Ye Olde H's." Here's why. After Charlie Herren sold his remaining interest to Guido, he returned to downtown Atlanta with another Herren's Restaurant ("Back by popular demand"). People were confused, and remained so. Guido consulted an attorney who was one of our regulars, but was told, "How can you prove he's hurting your business? You've got them standing in line and he's empty."

That year Duncan Hines felt it appropriate to advise his legions of readers to be sure to go to the old Herren's Restaurant, which was one of his recommendations for many years. So to differentiate the two restaurants, puckish Guido had a tiny neon sign made to go above our marquee. It transformed Herren's into Ye Olde Herren's. Later, one of Amalia's managers was looking for an appropriate logo and came across the New England town crier we used for years afterward.

Still later, with Mr. Herren's other place long gone and Guido gone to the Great Dining Room in the Sky, we hired a decorator. He saw the "Ye Olde" and the town crier logo, and we ended up with an Old New England decor, complete with a wallpaper mural of Newburyport, Massachusetts on one large wall. That wallpaper became the back page of our lunch menus and, in self defense, I learned a good bit about the buildings pictured on it.

In 1973, Atlanta's famous "anonymous donor" gave Atlanta a splendid present. All the property from the Candler Building south to Edgewood Avenue between Peachtree and Pryor Streets was leveled and turned into Central City Park. The area was bisected by a short block of Auburn Avenue, which was realigned to connect it with Luckie Street, adding still another name change to our street. Auburn Avenue (they called it "Sweet Auburn") was the locus of the black business district, containing the Wheat Street Baptist Church, Ebenezer Baptist Church, the Martin Luther King Center, the Royal Peacock Club, and other prominent landmarks. Nowadays the area is called the Fairlie-Poplar District, named after the intersection of two streets at the opposite corner of our block. The purpose of this discussion is to point out the centrality of the location along with the profusion of restaurants in the area.

Thanks to our great homegrown architect and developer, John Portman (a graduate of Tech High School, which shared the campus with Boys' High and Georgia Tech), our town has grown northward. Our guests, who were members of firms that moved from the Fulton Bank Building two blocks south to Peachtree Center four blocks north, were lost to us. One of our radio ads recognized this situation, suggesting that the health conscious could stroll to Herren's from Peachtree Center, eat lunch, and top it off with a piece of our famous lemon ice box pie, and jog back to Peachtree Center. (While the ad didn't bring any business, someone com-

plained about our use of the Peachtree Center name in the ad. I
hope we slip by here.)

As people moved out of our area we were, at first, not alarmed,
feeling the offices they left behind would soon be occupied by new
tenants. To a degree this was true, but gradually our business began
to erode. When the Forsyth Building across the street was replaced
with a parking lot as was the Dinkler Hotel and the Knight's Table
(old Ship Ahoy) Restaurant, we added a new twist to our advertising. "Lighted parking, directly across the street." We still had our
lobster tank, but we were not the only ones. And it had problems,
too. We joined with other distressed folks in our industry and sub-
scribed to the prominent two-fer club. This brought tremendous
customer counts, plenty of business for our servers, steadier work for
our kitchen staff, and even money for our landlord, who had a percentage lease. But it didn't mean much in the bottom line.

We even printed a $10 giveaway coupon in the local papers.
While we were setting it up, I realized we were printing millions of
dollars' worth of coupons and I imagined lines of people going out
of sight down the street, all with coupon in hand! Later I was told
one of our servers bought extra copies of that paper and kept
coupons in her pocket, which she would use to reward her guests
who didn't happen to have a coupon. In turn, I was told, she hoped
for a monetary benefit. The best laid plans . . .

As a silly aside here, I've always believed that our city should
have recognized those of us in this two-fer program for the great
service we provided to the city. Atlanta grew outward, with many
merchants moving to the malls, and offices moving to new office
parks and buildings in the suburbs. Downtown became more and
more deserted. People were afraid to come downtown for dinner.
Why should they bother, when there were so many good eating
places in the 'burbs?

The two-fers promotion took Atlanta by storm. I am confident that some suburban low-priced eateries bit the dust because they couldn't compete. People came to us from the suburbs and many surrounding towns to join in the two-fer frenzy. They came to town, had a good meal, spent less money than they would have in their own area (even if a place like any of ours was available), and went safely home. When conversations with their friends got around to food, they might mention that they had come downtown and dined at Herren's the previous weekend. "Weren't you afraid to go into the big town at night like that?" they might be asked. Would our guests have said, "Yes, I was afraid, but I got one steak free"? Of course not! They had to say, "It was great and it was perfectly safe. Atlanta is clean and well lighted at night and is a great place." Well . . . it could be, couldn't it?

Somewhere I used to keep a figure of how many people we served during that promotion. Maybe someday I'll look it up. I believe that those people were great ads for downtown Atlanta. Well, I can dream, can't I?

Do-It-Yourself Restaurant Guide

Consider this chapter as the beginnings of what might be a "how to" book on restaurant operation. It isn't because that's a subject for a complete college education. I'm just trying to give you a little flavor of the food service industry along with a view of some aspects never considered by diners.

Today there's a virtual explosion of new restaurant openings. Statistics show that pitifully few of these newcomers will be in business even a year later. Most successful new operations are expansions by well-run companies or franchises, but they're not immune to problems either. One of the best-run fern bar places near my home is rumored to be on the block. Its guests think the location is superb, but, unfortunately, there are not enough of them.

In general, independents that fail are the dream of someone without any restaurant experience who loves good food and has a pot of gold hidden nearby. Or someone who has had limited experience as a cook or maitre d' or what have you, but has never been totally in charge. Almost without fail, the undertaking is undercapitalized because there is too much optimism and not enough hardnosed attention to, or knowledge of, the facts of restaurant life. Most businessmen will tell you that theirs is the toughest business in the world. That may be so, but they might grudgingly change their minds if they consider the facts.

Every restaurant needs a good location with plenty of its own parking, high visibility, and low rent from an accommodating land-lord in a building right smack in the center of an area where every-one is going to love you. Since all those things rarely exist in the same spot, you'll have fun trying to decide which one or ones you can live without. (I once heard a landlord discussing a lease renewal tell a restaurateur that all he wanted was more. The restaurant was pay-ing a percentage lease so that the landlord was, in effect, a preferred partner in the business, being paid more and more as the business or inflation grew.)

On the other hand, you may be financially able or have the backing to buy the land, build your castle (including your huge parking lot), and equip the restaurant. (Have you considered simply investing all that moolah and retiring?) Continuing success requires that the location you select will only improve in desirability over the years required to retire all the debts.

You've already decided about your style of business. What kind of food? What price range? Who will be your Director of Food (chef) and how reliable will they be? How much will you have to pay to guarantee reliability? And what about sobriety?

And, of course, you're going to have a bar along with your beautiful dining room. That's an entire business by itself and even gets you into the entertainment business.

What will be the theme and the decor? Will you have carpets? Will you use tablecloths and, if so, what color and how big? Lots of people will want to rent linen to you, but which one will you use? How big will the tables be? Paper napkins or cloth? Candles . . . Big? Little? Wax? Electric? Liquid fuel? Buy? Rent? Where? Who's going to coordinate all this? And don't forget the chairs—there are hun-dreds of different ones to consider!

What kind of place setting will you use and how much back-up stock will you need? If you multiply (you don't even need a cal-culator for this one) your projected seats by the recommended number of pieces you should buy, you'll be overwhelmed. Where will you store all that china and silver? Never fear, if you buy too much, it will soon settle down to what you really need through breakage and pilferage.

Your manufacturing plant (for that is exactly what it is) will have to meet all kinds of special requirements to please the building inspector, the plumbing inspector, the fire inspector, the liquor regulatory agency, and the health department, not to mention the inspector from your insurance company (assuming you've found someone who will write insurance for you . . . it's all mandatory before opening). You are going to end up with the most expensive (per square foot) building on the block.

Don't forget outside signage. There's an inspector and lots of rules about that, too. The signs you really want will be too big for your lot or your pocketbook; maybe both. They can't be put where you want them, and someone will be upset if you prune any trees to make your place more visible.

Your occupancy expenses and maintenance costs will shock you. Before you even get started you'll have to make some hefty utility deposits, cash you won't see again for a long time. Early in your planning you should contact your *Yellow Pages* expert so that you might be in the phone book when you get started. It'll be another year before you get another chance.

You're going to pay big bucks to get someone to haul away your trash, most of which you just paid big bucks to haul in and store. And there are all kinds of rules about what you can do with the wastewater from your kitchen. Some of these may include regular visits from your plumber, whom you'll be calling from time to time anyway. You're going to hope you never see the plumber again . . . but you will.

Of course you've designed your menu to include all your favorite dishes plus those you believe your public wants. And you've designed your storage facilities with the right blend of dry storage, coolers, and freezers, including safe areas for all these goodies you'll be buying. By and large they're the same ones you and everyone else use at home. Don't forget to plan your building with the proper security against encroachment from the outside *and* the inside. Even the toilet paper isn't safe!

Your art department has been busy designing the new logo to go on your signs, advertising, and menus, and they've been negotiating with a printer to ensure that you'll have menus ready when you open. Make sure that you can change prices and offerings easily because you're going to find some prices too high or (horrors) too low and some dishes won't sell and your friends and guests will urge you to add their special favorites (but don't).

What about staff? How many servers, cooks, bartenders, dishwashers, salad makers, hostesses? What kind of pay for each? When will you start hiring and training? Do you know the federal regulations on pay in our industry? And what about OSHA records? Have you thought about benefits for these new employees . . . they're all going to want to know before they come on board. And, by the way, who's going to produce your payroll?

You'll have to make arrangements with credit card companies and arrange to install their machinery, some of which you may have to buy. You'll not only need supplies to run their system but you'll need space to store all the daily records they produce for the federally required length of time.

Have you and your accountant (surely you'd never think of starting without one, and don't go for someone with a cheap price!) decided on your cash handling practices and bookkeeping system. Who's going to handle all this? What kind of machinery will you use to ensure that all the food you buy and your cooks prepare gets to your guest's table and the money into your bank? What records will you be required to keep and store and for how long and where will you store them?

Who's going to watch the store while you're not there?

Who's going to help you while you are there?

If you're still with me, you've begun to realize that the restaurant business is a lot more complex than it seemed. You can always postpone the opening for a few more days to catch up on those things you forgot, assuming you know what they are. Interest charges keep running and income doesn't start . . . but you can delay.

Once you start the ball rolling the tiger is out of the cage—forever. Bills will pile up. Problems will crop up. It may rain or snow and nobody comes to lunch or dinner or both. Your newspaper ad has everything in it you wanted to say . . . but you forgot the address! (The paper won't; you'll get billed anyway!) Every publication, radio and TV station in town will be offering their services, they're all expensive, and each will convince you they are absolutely the best. And, considering the track record of new restaurants, all the advertising people will want cash in advance!

Once you start the ball rolling and the tiger roaming about at will, you've got to make decisions NOW. Assuming that everything goes perfectly for your opening, your operating problems begin, and they will never end as long as your doors are open.

I never kept a diary, but it is my impression that sinister forces have always gathered to make dire things happen at the most inappropriate times. You'd think I would have learned, but I'm like Charlie Brown trying to kick that football.

Anyway, just when you've forgotten the last time and are concentrating on other things, it's 4:00 P.M. on Friday afternoon and you're expecting big business on Friday and Saturday nights. (These things always happen at this time.) An employee asks, "What are we going to do about ice for dinner tonight?" You find out that both ice machines are empty, one since last night and the other since just after lunch today. Inspection shows that both machines are dead.

The ice vendor, whose plant is on the other end of town, says, "We'll get there as soon as we can." The repairman says, "Why do you guys always wait so late? I'm so tied up I can't get there until Tuesday."

Or you walk through the dish kitchen and happen to notice that the five-gallon pail of detergent serving the dishwashing machine is empty. You issue instructions to replace the empty pail. "We don't have any more," is the answer. "How long has that been that way?" you ask, afraid to hear the answer. "Since last Wednesday. We thought you knew and had ordered some more."

You start checking on your dinner server crew, which is already one short because of a sick child/dying grandmother/you name it, and you notice that someone else is missing. "Where's Lulu?" you ask, knowing that you have a full schedule of reservations and things are going to be tough with even one server missing. "Oh," someone volunteers, "she quit after lunch today. She told all of us last Monday that she was leaving today. We thought you knew."

And then there have been several sickening times when I realized at 12:15 that the house was full and the temperature was eighty-five degrees. Someone forgot to turn on the air conditioning. On a couple of those occasions it was machinery trouble, not repairable for two or three days. Even Mother Nature takes her toll from time to time. In 1987 we had one month when it rained at lunchtime for twenty-two straight days. I pictured my regulars falling like flies all over town from malnutrition!

A fairly common occurrence was well-publicized hoopla about a big convention coming to town. Everyone but me thought we would be super crowded, like in the good old days. Regular customers would tell me that they were going to skip that week because we'd be too crowded. I would beg and plead, "I can show you the books to prove it; we won't be busy next week. The conventioneers will be fewer in number than advertised. All their time will be planned." I would tell them. They wouldn't believe me. The staff would stare at each other and the four walls during convention week.

One time the convention planners even set up a kitchen and dining space in a local garage!

One week Atlanta was informed there would be 30,000 Shriners in town. Having been stuck with a lot of extra food by those folks who brought their own kitchen, I thought I should know more than I did. So I called the Shrine Temple to find out. I was told by the amiable gentleman in charge that while the total number was as accurate as could be determined at the time, this would not be a convocation of 30,000 people all at once. In fact, these fun lovers were coming from all over the state to compete in parade contests. A group would arrive on Monday morning, parade during the day, and return home by evening. On Tuesday, a different group would arrive and go through their paces. This was to last all week! Very few had time to eat in local restaurants or stay in local hotels. I was glad I'd made that call!

Though I have painted a bleak picture, owning a restaurant is an exciting and gratifying business. Most days most things go great. There are days that end with the last guest telling you what a fine meal he had, that you certainly have the best restaurant in the town/state/country/world, and he will certainly recommend you to all his friends. Over the years many thousands did just that.

However, I can't leave this area of discussion without telling you this story. One night I received a compliment from a late guest and went home overflowing with pompous and egotistical joy. I was happily contemplating the previous night's ending as I was walking from the parking lot to Herren's the next day when I noticed a letter posted on the door of one of my restaurant neighbors. Crossing the street to see what this notice said, I read, "This restaurant is closed. There will be a meeting of the creditors next Friday . . . ." As I reflected on the sudden demise of my neighbor, it occurred to me that someone had probably told him the same thing I had been told the night before, but today his business was gone. A sobering thought to start the day.

But don't take these musings as a reason to be discouraged or to quit. Rather, take them as a challenge. Get your training from experts in the industry and your financing from financial experts. Don't kid yourself about what you actually know and once you get started, keep kicking the ball!

Serving others is one of humankind's highest callings. It brings great rewards in self-satisfaction, and some have even found great financial blessings as restaurateurs.

Disaster

Once you show that you're willing to spend your time doing things other than pursuing your career, it's relatively easy to say "yes" and find yourself doing some volunteer work. Usually, people think of you in your field, decide that you are some kind of expert, and then flatter you into submission.

Such was the case when the Red Cross came to call. They knew that I had been in the restaurant business a long time, donated a lot of blood, and was obviously a sucker for a good deed project. Soooo, they asked me to serve on the Disaster Committee. My duty was to help see that volunteers were fed as they did their thing in pursuit of whatever sort of relief or help work was at hand.

Our first call was to support the search for a little boy who had fallen into Peachtree Creek in northeast Atlanta. I was amazed at the number of people who turned out to help. I don't believe that poor little fellow was found, at least not then nor in that area. But we set up the kitchen and fed the hungry.

Only a few weeks later, we were called on again in another area of town, the Hollywood Road area. The water involved was Proctor Creek, and the search again was futile.

Atlantans will recognize the diversity of the two areas involved, the first an affluent, though not super-wealthy neighborhood, the second a poorer area. In the second instance, we had just as many people actually working and searching, plus we had an extra contingent who came out for free eats and socializing. We had no problem with the free eats, though we had to raid a nearby grocery store for more supplies. It was the socializing that got out of hand. As darkness fell, someone built a fire and someone else thought it might be interesting to add some noise. When someone told me the noise was coming from bullets thrown on the fire I went looking for a phone.

Though it was after hours, I knew the mayor's secretary and where to reach her. I always liked to start at the top. I told her what we were doing and that we needed police protection. Within minutes we had all the police we needed and then some. See, it pays to start at the top.

Not many weeks later, the racial unrest around the country came to Atlanta in the form of riots near the stadium area. We heard about it on the radio and saw it on TV. Atlantans will remember pictures of Mayor Ivan Allen, Jr. (another Boys' High boy) courageously standing on a police car, addressing the crowd.

While we were watching all this on TV, the phone rang and Beautiful Jane handed it to me. It was none other than the mayor's secretary. "We've got 500 (or some such number) police officers down at the stadium to control things, and it's time to feed them. Call your Red Cross buddies and get to work!" When she finally accepted the idea that I didn't control the Red Cross or even know where to start, she came back with, "But you're the food man and these men are hungry and need to be fed."

"Can't you open some school cafeterias and get their help to prepare sandwiches?" I asked. "We don't control them, and we can't do that," she said. "It's up to you to do something." Well!

Racking my wife's brain, I finally called the Varsity, which Atlantans know as the world's largest and most splendiferous drive-in. The stories you can hear about the place are endless, entertaining, and probably all true. "Sells more Coca-Cola than any other one spot in the world, has no cash control system, collects all the money in gallon mayonnaise jars."

Mr. Gordy (Frank, the owner and originator, said to be a dropout from Georgia Tech in the '20s and one of the world's Great People) was not available so I talked to his manager. I explained the problem. He simply said "What do you need, and when can you pick it up?"

I ordered 300 hamburgers, 300 of their famous chili dogs, 300 fried apple pies, 300 fried peach pies, and enough french fries to bury the Queen Mary. "I'll be there in about thirty minutes."

"It'll be ready," was his laconic reply.

I called Mr. Allen's secretary and told her that I was on the way, but that I didn't really care to make the delivery alone. "I'll have a police escort meet you in front of City Hall."

When I arrived at the Varsity and identified myself, everything went like clockwork as if this were an entirely normal operation. The food, ready and in boxes, was loaded into my car with no delay.

At City Hall the escort (two police cars!) was waiting as promised and led me to the stadium where I unloaded and beat a hasty retreat, but not before I noted a police car with a very large bullet hole in its side.

This story was brought to mind a few years ago when John Costello, one of son Paul's friends, came to visit. He reminded me that he was present when I called the Varsity, but not before. I didn't realize that he had heard only one side of the conversation. No wonder his chin hit his chest and his eyes bugged out on stems when he heard me place the order. Of course, Jane explained what was happening as I shot out the back door on my mission of mercy.

From time to time over the ensuing years, we have had numerous occasions with John to reminisce and join in hearty laughter. He maintains this is his most "mind boggling" experience. Mine too!

Are We Insured?

I n my early restaurant days, and before the great post-war explosion of dining-out facilities, I became well aware that the clientele my father had brought to Herren's did not, even then, care to come to town to eat dinner. They belonged to exclusive clubs or they could afford servants to prepare their meals at home.

At the same time, there were only a few large hotels in downtown Atlanta and the now-booming convention business was in its infancy. The hotels all had fine dining rooms and did all they could to keep their guests inside. Additionally, there was the bar situation.

Atlanta, and for that matter Georgia, was technically dry as far as mixed drinks were concerned. As in many jurisdictions across the country the politicians were said to "drink wet and vote dry." Beer and wine were okay to serve but mixed drinks were not . . . technically. Everybody served them but with differing levels of managerial neuroses regarding visits from the constabulary. In this atmosphere, sometimes we served good mixed drinks to always thirsty dinner guests, sometimes the drinks were watered down to a certain alcohol content because of industry rumors of impending crackdowns, and sometimes (when the "word" was out) we served only beer, wine, and apologies to angry strangers.

Serving drinks was against the law, but on election days it was even more so! When the polls closed at 7:00 P.M. we generally started serving. Private clubs and some hotels seemed exempt from this paranoia and went ahead with liquor service, or so we heard.

Through all this we were constantly trying out differing strategies to lure Atlantans from the ever-widening suburbs. We served many regulars who stayed in town after a hard day at the office and were joined by their spouses for dinner and a movie at one of our five first-run downtown movie palaces. We also received sporadic support from the occupants of the nearby hotels as their attendance varied with goings-on in our town.

The late '40s and early '50s saw only aging and war-worn downtown hotels trying to compete with the new upstart in the hotel industry, the suburban motor hotels or motels. The word in those days was that there would never (!) be any new hotels built downtown. John Portman and I were both much younger then! Against this background of outside forces and ever-changing factors, we continued to do business in the heart of the business district. Lunch business was good, but dinner business was never consistent and only rarely exceptional.

Prodded by our faithful local dinner guests and encouraged by my beautiful wife, who always seemed to have the best advice, I decided to take the plunge and specialize in Maine lobsters.

Maine lobsters have always been an expensive entree. Unlike most other foods that are produced by man's manipulation of the earth's bounties, Maine lobsters have stoutly resisted man's constant desire for more of the best and his proclivities for thwarting the rules of Mother Nature.

To start with, in all the world, Maine lobsters are found only in the North Atlantic. All other oceans boast some form of the spiny lobster, that, unlike its cousin from the north, has no claws. (Instead it has two long spiny feelers.) It is known alternatively as the Florida, Cuban, or African lobster and only the tail contains edible meat.

This, of course, makes the supply of Maine lobsters limited. Three other factors contribute to the high producer cost of lobsters:

1. They grow very slowly . . . a one-pound lobster is about five years old.
2. Catching them is still, for our consideration, a one-at-a-time activity in a trap in all kinds of weather, and those caught must be stored (in ponds) for the out-of-season months.
3. The advent of the jet age and improved packaging enlarged the potential market from the railroad-served eastern seaboard to practically the entire world.

Now that you know more than you ever wanted to about the subject you might begin to wonder what made us think of specializing in this delicacy back in 1958. Because no one else was doing it, we felt that we could be successful if we did things correctly.

Having made this decision, we ordered Atlanta's very first lobster tank from a firm in St. Louis and anxiously awaited its arrival. When it failed to arrive, the manufacturer supposedly shipped another. When it eventually arrived it turned out to be the first one that was shipped. It had been sitting around a truck terminal for months because nobody knew what it was and could not identify it when inquiries were made!

Some years later, when I was on the Board of Directors of the National Restaurant Association, I met a fellow board member from St. Louis who had designed this particular tank. He was a mechanical engineer restaurateur who built the first one for his own restaurant. I never got real chummy with him, but upon learning that I was the guy from Atlanta who bought his tank he commented, "Oh, you're the one!"

But what a monster I had created! I averaged at least one hour each day working on the tank and frequently said, "I want to be buried in it." After I played nursemaid to this mechanical marvel for many years, *Atlanta Journal* columnist Ernie Rogers dubbed me "Atlanta's Lobstertrician!"

When everything went right, we displayed ninety gallons of

sparkling clear (filtered down to three microns, for you engineers) refrigerated seawater. The pH, salinity, and temperature had to be correct because the lobsters knew the difference and promptly died if things were not right. We learned the hard way (fifty untimely deaths into the garbage) that precautions must be taken when using insect spray. Hundreds of undreamed-of problems and pitfalls.

But people came to town to enjoy fresh lobster. They knew the lobster was fresh because they were allowed to choose the one they wanted to eat. An occasional problem arose when the cooks had several orders at a time and someone would complain, "This is not the one I picked. Mine was a female and this one is a male!" And you thought it only made a difference to the lobsters! (You might be interested to know that there is more meat in the tail of a female and the true aficionado can recognize the broader tail in the tank.)

As you can imagine, if you have stuck with me to here, there must be many lobster stories. I'll tell you a few. But to begin, I must tell you that in all my years I never had many complaints about our food. The fact that we lasted so long and closed only after our part of town went down the tubes attests to the fact that we had mostly satisfied customers. Someone once told me, "You're not good because you're old, you're old because you're good." Before you think I'm talking about me, let me hasten to lay the credit where it is due . . . we had a great staff!

Before the advent of the tank, the complaints we had were generally about steaks that were tough or too fatty or too thin or not properly cooked—you name it. And they generally came from someone who would end up telling me, "I know all about meat. I used to work for Swift (or some other packer), and I'm an expert."

After the installation of the tank, everyone was a lobster expert because "I used to live in Maine." Some may have had legitimate complaints, and we were only learning the lore, but many were just plain full of baloney. A favorite complaint was, "You're too expensive. I can get that same lobster in Maine for $1.50," to which I occasionally replied—if pushed far enough—that it only cost $100 for a round trip ticket to Maine on Eastern Air Lines to take advantage of that bargain, and that's the way our lobsters came to us.

We had cleared a spot in our front window for the tank, where it generated great attention from passersby. The local newspaper ran a page-wide strip of pictures of people looking at something (my family was in one of the pictures—by happenstance) with the caption, "What Are They Looking At?? See Page 6." Of course, Page 6 had a close-up of a lobster in our tank.

Occasionally the tank would be empty, and we would display just water, sparkling clear and bubbling. On one such occasion we made a small sign that was visible from the sidewalk. It said: "This tank full of rare invisible tropical fish." I lost count of how many people stood outside studying the water intently and pointing to what they must have imagined were those rare fish . . . suddenly catching on to the joke. Some burst out laughing and others looked around furtively, hoping no one was watching.

During one particularly good fishing season, the price of lobsters went so low that we decided to have an unusual promotion on our usually slow Thursday nights (reputed to be the "maid's night out" in Atlanta). We called it simply Lobster Night and advertised it heavily.

For the promotion we offered a chicken lobster (1-1/8 pound, the smallest that could be shipped from Maine) dinner for $1.95, two for $3.85, and three for $5.75. The response was overwhelming! On those Thursday nights we served from 250 to 350 lobsters, sometimes more. An amusing aside to this promotion was the comment of our long-time chef, Johnny Dunn, who told me one day he had so many live lobsters on his work station at one time that, "It was the first time in my life I've ever had the food crawling off my work table!" Years after this promotion was long over I still had people telling me that they saw the ad in the paper "just last week!"

Early on in the tank era we provided cloth bibs for our guests. A problem quickly surfaced: our guests wanted to take them home, and many did (and they cost us two bucks apiece). Laundering them was a real problem. Our regular laundry, accustomed to only napkins and tablecloths, was unable to do a satisfactory job. For a while we would take them home (until my Beautiful Jane rebelled) and then we took them to a neighborhood laundry. Ultimately we succumbed to the least of many evils and started using disposable plastic bibs.

When the tank was full it usually contained about fifty 1-3/4 pound lobsters. For some reason, suspected by me but known only to the lobsters themselves, they would always pile on top of each other in the four corners of the tank so that the backs of some of them would be out of water. On more than one occasion, this practice resulted in one of their number actually making it over the side of the tank and onto the floor.

When the tank was thus filled, it was not unusual to see an unpegged claw sticking up from the water, slowly opening and then snapping shut. I've got to tell you that I have seen such action easily and almost instantly snap a wooden pencil in two. On one such occasion, I noted a rather tall, extremely well endowed and beautiful young lady leaning over the edge of the tank for a better look at a lobster on the far side. Nothing overt happened but the episode got me to thinking and I called my insurance agent, Bill Leide, son of the late maestro, Enrico Leide.

Bill was one of my regulars and understood immediately when I explained the situation. "Does my insurance cover it if that young lady gets caught by a lobster?" "Only if I get to inspect the damage," he replied.

Coats

Over these many years, owning a restaurant has been a great opportunity to observe a fascinating diversity of behavior of humans faced with a variety of everyday problems.

At Herren's we had an unattended coat room in the upstairs lobby and a less formal situation of hanging rods and hat racks on two walls in the lower lobby. The word "unattended" is the key to this story. In recent years people have become more protective of their possessions and are less inclined to leave them in such a room, but people were more trusting not too many years ago.

In the old days (maybe even the good old days) men left their coats in our coat room. (Ladies! Don't chastise me for talking about men's coats. You've always been too smart to leave yours in such a situation!)

Somewhere near the middle to the end of our lunch period we occasionally became aware that someone was searching frantically and unsuccessfully for his coat. When lunch was over that day, we invariably had a coat left over, along with the name of the searcher.

Early in the life of this particular coat room it became obvious what was happening. Mr. A would go into the room, coat in hand. Seeing the expanse of hanging space, he might briefly wonder how he would find his coat among the many when he had finished his lunch. After all, in those days most men's coats looked almost exactly alike. Being a thoughtful captain of industry, the man would hang his coat on the end of the rack or at least right next to a divider.

Next came Mr. B, equally perplexed as to the recovery of his coat. "Aha! I'll hang it on the end." By the time the room was full and Mr. A was ready to depart, his coat would have been pushed down the line, perhaps even to the end, but surely not where he left it.

Now having paid his tab and being somewhat in a hurry, Mr. A grabs what he thinks is his coat (after all it *looks* like his coat—black London Fog, red lining, hanging on the end of the rack) and he heads off to the office, where there is no competition for hanging space, and then home.

By the time the owner of the coat Mr. A innocently purloined (he may be Mr. X, Y, or Z) comes for his coat, he might repeat this scenario for a three-way swap, or, because he was one of the last to arrive and depart, he might easily detect that his coat is gone. Sometimes the remaining coat would have identification. (We used to give out coat tags for this purpose and many would install them on an extra inside button.) Mr. B might wear the remaining coat home and end up owning a coat better than the one he lost.

Or we might solve the mix-up when Mr. A sheepishly calls the next day. He might confess that he took the wrong coat. Then again, if he's aggressive enough, he may say someone took his! By this time you get the picture. Coats get swapped. Innocently. And sometimes irrevocably. I never did locate the five-foot-tall man who left his coat and took one that belonged to a six-foot-six giant.

One blustery winter day I was standing in the lobby discussing the very situation I described above. *It* had happened again, and I was doing my foot-scuffling act, trying to mollify one of my guests. In such a situation, I have been known to lend my own coat to the injured party just to get him back to his office.

As we talked, a tall, distinguished-looking gentleman entered the lobby and could not help but overhear my blathering. I finished as he was removing his coat, a beautiful camel colored cashmere that obviously was extremely expensive. Something prompted him to enter our conversation with, "I don't have that problem since there are not many coats like mine," after which he disappeared into the coat room (to hang his coat on the end?). He did not witness the arrival of the next two guests, who were both wearing coats identical to his.

Another time I was in the lower lobby and the meal period had progressed enough that the racks were well filled. The joiner-into-the-conversation announced he had no problem recognizing his coat among the others. He simply tied a knot in the sleeve before he hung it up, a feat he proceeded to demonstrate. About five minutes after Mr. Knot was seated I noticed another gentleman in the lobby going through the coats until he spotted his, he thought. Suddenly he exclaimed, "Who the hell tied a knot in the sleeve of my coat?"

Another method down the drain.

On still another rainy day, I found a prominent Atlantan looking through the coats in the downstairs lobby. "Mine was very much like this one," he said, indicating (what else?) a black London Fog with a red lining. I assured him that an error had been made and that I thought I knew everyone who had already left that day (slow business . . . rainy day) and that I would call them all. Since it was the only BLFWRL on the rack, he declared that he was going to wear it to the office and bring it back the next day (against my advice, I might add, since it might just precipitate a three-way problem).

Well, to make a long story longer, we had no three-way, but he did bring the coat back the next day. A very close examination of the coat under bright light revealed a very faint name with initials . . . someone I did not know but have since met. Sure enough, the name was in the phone book, and sure enough it was his coat . . . but that's not the end of the story. "He's had my coat for about two

53

weeks. I had a late lunch at the Commerce Club and when I was ready to leave there was only one coat in the coat room. It was similar to mine, only a lot newer," he continued. "The manager said I was the only one in the club and insisted I wear that coat home, which I did. I took it back the next day and it has resided in the manager's office ever since, and I've been without a coat. I'm coming to Herren's tomorrow to have lunch and pick up my coat, and you can tell him to go to the Commerce Club and get his own damn coat!"

By now you have discerned that someone might take the wrong coat from among many and not realize it at the time. If he merely picks up "his" coat (at home or at the office), he may not be aware of the swap.

Over the years all kinds of things were left and never claimed, eventually given away to the employee who found and turned it in or to some deserving guest. One day a male friend shook a very feminine looking umbrella at me and said, "This is the one you gave me a year ago after mine showed up missing . . . and I've had it ever since!"

One more sad tale and I'll let you go.

One night about 11:00, as the last party in the house was about to leave, one of the two men imperiously demanded that I produce his hat. "I had one when I came in, and I put it in the coat room. Now it's gone, and I'm not leaving without my hat."

"But sir," I explained patiently, "if it's not there I can't produce it. Please leave your name and phone number and I'll investigate tomorrow and call you."

"I'm not leaving without my hat. I came in with it, and I'm not leaving without it!"

"Maybe you left it at your table . . . I'll go and search the dining room." No luck. No hat. I even checked the rest room.

"I'm the president of the XYZ Company of Baltimore and I'm

not leaving without my hat!!"

"But sir, it's 11:30 and everyone's gone and your hat's not here."

"I don't care, I want my hat!"

I don't know how you would have handled this, but I finally called the police. A very polite sergeant appeared almost instantly, listened to my story, and advised the man to leave quietly.

"I'm not going, I want my hat!" His dinner companion had patiently suffered through all this, occasionally urging him, "Let's go on back to the hotel. We can settle this tomorrow." Now he took Mr. President by the arm and dragged him out the door.

What a way to end a long day!

End of story? Not quite. The next day I received a call from the companion who apologized for his friend and asked if the man had called me. When I said that he had not, my caller said, "Well, I'm sorry he didn't call, but I will apologize for him and tell you that when we returned to the hotel his hat was right there on the bed, where he had left it."

When you're in a public business, you see all kinds.

Mom's Apple Pie

How many ways can you offer items on your menu? Restaurateurs through the years have pondered this problem *ad nauseam*. The limitation is related to the number of adjectives in the English language plus those few imported from other languages. Regardless of how good your products are, your guest only sees what's on the menu. That's why many modern menus show mouthwatering full color pictures and many places display their desserts in a refrigerated glass case. The really fancy places have the dessert cart or the tray, offered by your server in person.

Many years ago, Atlanta had a very fine restaurant called Mammy's Shanty, owned by Floridian Charles Creighton and operated by my friend Preston Weeks. Mr. Creighton operated in Florida with large signs proclaiming, "The World's Best Apple Pie." When he bought the Shanty, he added that slogan to the sign and his apple pie to the menu. This story does not address itself to the appropriateness of that slogan; everyone has an opinion about what tastes best. Suffice it to say that his pie was powerfully good by my taste test, even though I preferred ours just a tad more.

In our town at that time was another entrepreneur named Tom Ham, who was one of God's gifts to comedy. He and his partner operated a number of places called Seven Steers with a hilariously funny menu and decor. When Tom saw Mr. Creighton's sign he could not resist it. His menu immediately offered, "The World's

Roundest Apple Pie." Not to be outdone, another restaurant whose name escapes me jumped on the bandwagon with "The World's Flattest Apple Pie."

As we sat pondering this flurry of one-upmanship, someone said just the right thing at the right time and we changed our menu. We offered "The World's Second Best Apple Pie." By now you should know that I would never knock the competition. In fact, I never considered other restaurateurs to be the competition. Our real competitors in the food business were good cooks at home and the A&P. Nevertheless, that second best stuff needed an explanation. We instructed our staff on the proper response to anyone who asked, "If yours is second best, whose is first?"

We taught our folks that they should never, ever, ever tell a guest something that was not true. In fact, they were taught to say "I don't know" if they didn't know and then try to find out the answer from someone who did know, and communicate that.

My answer to that question is, "Mom's Apple Pie is best," and I quickly added, "Your mom's, not mine."

Those who knew of my Italian heritage might have appreciated the subtle humor, others might think nostalgically of home. Still others might remember some mishap akin to my memory of Mamma trying to make doughnuts. She was a great cook, but her doughnuts were the origin of the word "sinkers."

While we're on the subject of apple pie, you've just got to hear about our best salesperson and apple pie.

One of our regular guests was Morris Hirsch, owner of Hirsch's Store for Men over on Peachtree Street. He usually was accompanied by members of his staff, but on this day he was alone. Lunchtime was over and almost everyone was gone when he sent for me and asked me to be seated. I was aware that he had been served by his regular waitress, Edna Neely, our gorgeous redhead.

"I came over here today to relax," he said, relating the trials and tribulations of the day. "I wasn't even hungry, but it seemed like a place to collect myself."

I listened patiently, sure he had some story to tell. I wasn't wrong.

"Edna convinced me that London broil was what I wanted, and it was excellent, even though I really wasn't hungry," he continued. "When I finished that, she started telling me about the hot apple pie that had just come up from the bake shop, how good it looked and smelled and how she was so sure that I needed some." Hearing this story, I was starting to get hungry!

"Well," he said, "just to be accommodating, I finally told her to bring a slice." I thought he had finished since it seemed to be a good enough story, but, without a moment's hesitation he added, "she continued, 'You want it a la mode, of course.'" Glory! A real selling job!

"As I ate my pie a la mode," Hirsch continues, "I reflected on what a great salesperson she was. Here I was, not even hungry, and she not only sold me dessert which I didn't need or want, but topped it off with an extra sale of ice cream. When I had finished my pie," he said, "I called her over and told her I wanted her to come to work for me at my store. She could go through the place," he said, "look at all the things we sold, and make up her own mind as to what she would like to sell. I told her I would build a special counter in the store just for her. It would be on the ground floor, just inside the front door right on Peachtree Street, so everyone who entered the store would see her first. She thanked me and asked, 'Can I sell apple pie a la mode?'"

I'm happy to report that she continued selling apple pie a la mode for us for many years and retired after twenty-five years, just as beautiful as ever.

But the subject was desserts.

And speaking of Herren's desserts, we made an absolutely

splendiferous lemon ice box pie with graham cracker crust. After admitting to second best on the apple pie, we claimed world's best for the lemon. When asked for the recipe, which happened at least once a week from guests and twice from *Gourmet Magazine* (which we ignored for obvious reasons), we referred them to the recipe on the Eagle Brand Sweetened Condensed Milk can. It was pretty close if you double or tripled everything. (Note: I just gave you the recipe for our Lemon Pie!)

We served a huge slice of this super rich confection for thirty cents. Our most common comment about our food was about our lemon pie. "It's too good," "It's too much," or "It's too rich." Those who knew what it was they were ordering would usually order one slice and split it between two.

One day we realized that while we had been following the cost of other commodities, our cost of this delightful dessert was approaching 100% of our sales price. Something had to be done. Raise the price, of course. I never met a restaurant man who wasn't concerned about raising prices. There were guests who watched our prices like hawks and took a five-cent raise as a personal affront. One regular, a personal friend, took such umbrage at price changes that he would stay away for weeks (still a powerful way to punish your neighborhood restaurateur who has done you wrong).

Determined to assuage my friend's financial hurt, I would watch for him whenever we found it necessary to change prices. I would spend time with him, talking of his favorite subjects and maybe even slipping in a word or two about my problem. When he finished, I would pick up his check with a flourish, saying that it had been my pleasure to have been able to spend some time with him. I more than covered his extra nickels for many, many weeks and hoped that his continued regular attendance would more than make up for the occasional free meal. I tried it more than once because I really liked this fellow, but it never worked.

Back to the lemon pie.

We decided that, rather than raise the price, we would cut the pie into eight slices instead of six, thus raising our income to $2.40 instead of $1.80. After all, everyone said that we served too much. Well, I'm here to tell you that they were kidding. They *loved* those big, rich slices and they were mad as hell when we cut the size. Three days was enough. We returned to the six-cut pie and raised the price to forty cents. Not a word from anyone.

Several weeks after this, one of my regulars dropped by to say hello during the afternoon. Over a cup of coffee he told me that he had watched the "lemon pie ballet" and had a suggestion. "For those who still think one-sixth cut is too big, offer them a half-slice for twenty-five cents. The worst loss will be that you'll have a half slice left over at the end of a meal, and you'll now be getting fifty cents for what you used to sell for thirty cents!" Well, we tried it. They liked it. From then on, our menu offered the half slice, the most popular size by far!

And still speaking of lemon pie . . .

One of my regular guests told me he had tried to bring his wife and two young sons to Herren's the previous week on Thanksgiving Day. We were always closed on such holidays, since our principal clientele at lunchtime was businessmen who were at home on the holidays. Finding us closed, he walked his family up the street to Leb's. "As we were walking through the restaurant," he said, "one of my sons shouted, 'But I want to go to Herren's so I can eat some of their good lemon pie!'"

Well, a couple of "sweet roll" stories will round out this section.

Standing at the cash stand one day, I noted a beautiful and very well dressed lady paying her check. I knew she had eaten alone, and I expressed surprise that her bill was almost $20, almost double our lunch check average. When I commented on the possibility that there was an error, she smiled and told me that she had bought some sweet rolls to take home.

"I'm from Washington, D.C., and I've been in Atlanta for three days," she said. "I've eaten here every day and have become addicted to your sweet rolls. I'm taking six dozen back with me." I told her I was happy she had been with us and hoped that she had a safe journey home and would come back again. I also asked her not to tell the FDA, DEA, FBI or anyone else that she had become "addicted" to the sweet rolls. "Just tell them how good they are, and leave out that word!"

A few weeks after Herren's closed, one of my regulars called and invited me to have lunch with his usual bunch of guys. They were a group of college fraternity men who had been having lunch together at Herren's on Thursdays for more years than any of us could remember. I was delighted to attend, even though I am not a member of their fraternity. One of the "boys" told me that even though his office was downtown, he frequently worked out of town for five or six months at a time. During the last period away, he told me, he had hungered for Herren's sweet rolls and had arranged with his secretary to ship two dozen to him every week. She would regularly appear at our cash desk and order two boxes of a dozen sweet rolls, pay for them, and leave. None of us could recall her as a guest; we had wondered who the mystery lady was.

I can't leave this section without one more apple pie story. I like to call it . . . *Ellen Pie.*

When our daughter Ellen was three or four years old, Jane would do her hair in side ponytails. She'd even used her scissors to alter a hat so the ponytails could stick out. Many a mother would exclaim, "How darling! Wherever did you find such a cute hat?"

Sometimes Jane brought our brood downtown to join me for dinner. The kids always felt at home in the restaurant, and our employees would watch over them when, from time to time, they would wander off on their own explorations. We always sat by the front door, at the table we could never sell, so I could stick to my job and still visit with my family.

On one particular evening, as a regular guest was leaving, he stopped at our table to chat. He said that as he was eating his dinner and reading his paper, he became aware that someone was staring at him. Lifting his eyes, he noted a little pixie barely tall enough to see over the top of the table. It was Ellen, peering intently at him. He greeted her and tried to make small talk.

Suddenly she said, "You're eating *two* pieces of pie!"

He explained that, in order to spend as little time as possible at dinner, he always ordered the entire meal to be brought to his table at the same time. "And she caught me this time," he said, "I *was* eating two pieces of your delicious apple pie."

Sweet Rolls & Other Stuff

Talk to anyone about Herren's and somewhere in the conversation they will invariably mention sweet rolls or cinnamon buns or sticky buns. If you never tasted Herren's sweet rolls, mere words will not suffice to educate you. If you have, make up your own words. I've made up my mind to include the recipe with this writing, but I want to tell you a few stories first.

Years ago, in the early days of Herren's, someone made the first sweet roll and placed it in a basket of hot Parker House rolls. Nothing has been the same since. In my early days, while I was still experimenting and learning about the business, I came to realize that our guests were not buying our great homemade desserts, made fresh each day in our own bakery. (We produced Strawberry Boston Cream Pie, Chocolate Ice Box Cake with Whipped Cream, Mincemeat Pie with Wine Sauce, and many, many more.) We were proud of these goodies and received many compliments from our guests who were willing and able to spend an extra thirty cents. Our employees, including me, loved them. Most of our guests, dessert lovers all, eschewed them. Instead, they would cagily order more sweet rolls in the middle of their meals and save them for dessert to accompany their unlimited coffee refills.

This seemed unsportsmanlike to me, and I decided to do something about it. My solution was to stop making sweet rolls, using the excuse that our baker was out sick. The reaction from our guests was so violent that I not only restored the sweet rolls but worked out a system to provide them in quantity even if our baker was away. Our daily dessert specials went by the wayside, and I learned a valuable lesson. Don't mess with the sweet rolls!

In recent years, the city of Atlanta completed a downtown improvement project and local merchants were asked to join in the celebration. Called The Broad Street Bash, it was a two-day (Thursday and Friday) outdoor festival centered on that part of Broad Street that now was an entrance plaza for the new Metropolitan Atlanta Rapid Transit Authority (MARTA) Five Points Station.

We joined in the festivities by operating a small booth in which we offered Herren's Delicious Sweet Rolls. We offered a sealed plastic bag containing six sweet rolls for $1 (we were selling them in the restaurant for $1.50 a dozen at the time). The price was designed to make change-making simple. We had no idea what would happen.

Our plan was to have one person operating the booth, one person running supplies to the booth (about four blocks from Herren's), one person packing the bags, and our wonderful baker concentrating on making more, a tedious hand process. We thought we had all the bases covered, but our booth was swamped with orders, and never without a line when our runner arrived with more rolls.

During all this madness we were still serving lunch as usual at Herren's. Almost from the first few minutes it became apparent that we had bitten off a large chunk of problems. Even though we had planned ahead with a huge backlog from the day before, ready to bake off, and had started at 5:00 A.M. that day, our inventory of sweet rolls was rapidly depleted. Someone had to help the baker, so we promoted the person doing the packaging to baker's assistant. Someone had to fill in for the packager. I took this spot and let the hostesses run the dining rooms. Someone had to help seal the packages because the packaging job made for sticky fingers, not suitable for handling and sealing. We used a busboy who could double as an additional runner. Our manager was already out of the building, manning our booth on Broad Street, a job where I relieved him later in the day, when the frenzy began to abate.

My packaging job involved using a large spatula to lift six sweet rolls from the baking pan and insert them into the plastic bag. Simple enough when the rolls were cool, but increasingly messy as the inventory became smaller and the pans and rolls became warmer and gooier. Inevitably some rolls broke, leaving random pieces of cinnamon/sugar/butter delight behind in the pan. After snacking on the first little morsel, I was hooked and continued to eat a sweet roll here and there as work continued.

All participants were exhausted by the end of the day. My sugar binge resulted in a five-pound weight gain, and Atlantans gave us all a rousing reception.

Mercifully, it rained on Friday.

Since the sweet rolls were basically a bread product they had a fairly long shelf life even though no preservatives were ever used. We sold them hot by the dozen to those who wanted them for their afternoon coffee break, or frozen in aluminum pans with printed covers. One of my friends took a dozen boxes with him to Ireland, where he proudly distributed them as gifts from Atlanta.

I was always free with the sweet roll recipe because it is not so much a recipe as an assembly direction. Several books contain this recipe, and it has been printed in the Atlanta newspapers on numerous occasions. Several days after one printing we received an anguished call from a lady who said, "It says to turn the dough out on a floured board. When I do that it runs off the edges onto the floor!"

We reviewed the recipe, which shows 1/4 cup of warm water, but never says that this is for dissolving the yeast. The newspaper recipe read "1-1/4 cups of warm water" No wonder!

So popular were these rolls and so frequent the recipe request that we published it ourselves as a giveaway. Our waxed take-home bag conveyed this treasured information. For many years this recipe went home with every take-out purchase; the bag was also used as our doggy bag. To celebrate our forty-fifth anniversary we handed out one of these bags with a dozen hot sweet rolls to everyone who dined with us on that day.

Herren's closing was noted on the front of the Metro section of *The Atlanta Journal/Constitution* on November 14, 1987. We served our last meal on Friday the 13th, always a significant date in the Negri family. That story carried this recipe, which has appeared in those pages another time since our closing.

Sweet Rolls from Herren's

1 cup milk	1/4 cup warm water
1/4 cup butter	4 cups flour, sifted
1/4 cup sugar	Cinnamon/sugar mixture:
1-1/4 teaspoons salt	2 cups sugar
2 packages yeast	4 Tablespoons cinnamon

Let milk come to a boil in heavy saucepan. Add butter, sugar and salt. Cool. Soften yeast in 1/4 cup warm water and stir into first mixture. Add flour, about half at a time, and beat well. Turn out on a floured board, allow to sit for 15 minutes, then knead until smooth.

Place dough in a buttered bowl, cover with a cloth, and let rise until double in size.

Roll out dough about 1/4 inch thick on a floured board and cut into roughly 8-inch squares. Working one square at a time, brush with melted butter and sprinkle cinnamon and sugar mixture generously over entire surface. Starting at one side of the square, roll up

66

into a tube. Continue rolling tube back and forth, stretching it sideways until it is 12 to 16 inches long. Cut tube into wheels approximately 1/2 inch wide. (Note: As this recipe will make 60 to 80 sweet rolls, use three or four small (6-inch to 8-inch) aluminum pans. This will allow you to stagger cooking during your dinner or refrigerate to bake for breakfast.) Place sweet rolls in pan that has been thoroughly buttered and coated with sugar/cinnamon mixture, so they touch, but don't over-pack. Brush top with melted butter and sprinkle generously with the sugar/cinnamon mixture over entire surface. Let stand at room temperature for one hour to rise. Please note that you have ended up with a confection of butter, sugar, and cinnamon, separated by a thin bit of dough.

Bake 18 to 20 minutes at 350 degrees. You may substitute your favorite yeast dough recipe or buy frozen dough from your supermarket. Minus the sugar, cinnamon, and butter, the dough can be used for Parker House or other dinner rolls.

From time to time people will call or write asking for a recipe for this dish or that. There are some famous stories about people asking for recipes from famous restaurants. Some received the recipes along with a substantial bill. (I believe the courts have ultimately ruled this payable.)

I always resisted most requests, not because of secrecy but because our recipes were for large quantities and I didn't have the time or expertise to reduce and test them. And even though a recipe might be followed accurately, the results might taste different at home.

Recently I bumped into a longtime customer/friend who reminded me I had promised but never given him our recipe for Thousand Island dressing. "Now that you are out of business I thought you might share this with me," he said.

I sent it to him with a letter saying, "This is a very old recipe out of our moldering files, but it is absolutely the one in use when you first tried it and were wowed. It is written in the original amounts, which yield about four gallons, so that you can see the original ingredients and their relationship to each other. Cut it down as you will to suit your taste or appetite."

His reply to me said, in part: "We made the entire quantity described therein, fed the whole neighborhood and had enough left over to seal our driveway. Ed, there will always be a warm spot in my heart for Herren's Restaurant . . . a few cases of heartburn notwithstanding!"

Integration—What Was It All About?

Our '60s really began in the '50s when it was time to sign another lease, my first experience at this activity. Our lunch business had grown to the point that we were filling our little sixty-seat downstairs room to capacity every day. Like the true, gutsy American entrepreneurs we thought we were, we hired a consultant who appeared on the scene in 1958.

His recommendations, though not followed to the letter, resulted in the remodeling and expansion that began in 1961 and ended in May of 1962. Between his visit, the resulting report, and the beginning of construction there was a lot of negotiating for the new lease, scraping for financing, planning and designing, bidding, rejecting, re-planning and—finally—a practically do-it-yourself project.

The lease negotiation itself is worth mentioning. Working through the landlord's agent, we weren't making any progress. Our lawyer, who knew everyone concerned, suggested we all sit down to dinner together and talk it over. So Beautiful Jane and I sat down with the landlord and his wife and had a wonderful evening. When it was over we realized for the first time that they really wanted us to continue as tenants. They told us that it dawned on them that we had no intention of moving and really wanted to sign a new lease.

Without closing for a single day, we finally had our two-level, 300-seat restaurant, capable of seating our lunch demand (about 600 on our best days), and a charming and cozy Williamsburg restaurant at dinnertime with 150 seats on the main level and a 150-seat banquet facility downstairs that became Herren's Gallery.

One new amenity was wool carpet where we had formerly had a checkerboard tile floor. On our very first day I noticed a guest using the public telephone by the front door. We had failed to supply an ashtray for his cigarette, which he casually dropped on our carpet and squashed underfoot. I was outraged and invited him to leave! I've often wondered how much my childish behavior cost us. (If he ever returned, though, I feel sure he didn't repeat that behavior.)

Our new carpet brought another problem. At the time, our sweet rolls included raisins, later to be eliminated forever when they became unavailable for a few months. Until that time, though, we endured constant complaints from our carpet maintenance people, who told us the ugly black spots were raisins that had been dropped and trampled into the rug.

Within weeks of our completion, the barricades went up around our neighbor, the Rialto Theater. The old building was torn down and a new one built while we watched our new carpet ground to shreds by the construction debris tracked in through the front and back doors! The raisin problem receded in importance and ultimately disappeared with the installation of more new carpet.

Many years later, in that theater's waning years, my friend Cecil Alexander, the architect, brought the color rendering of the projected new Rialto Theater to me, saying he thought I should have it. It showed a triangular marquee projecting out over the corner of Forsyth and Luckie Streets that advertised the film showing in the Rialto: *Cease Fire*, starring A. Lincoln.

Early 1963 brought a call from Ed Noble, a prominent developer who owned, among many other things, Yohannons, a very fine restaurant in Lenox Square. He issued a call to many of Atlanta's restaurateurs to have lunch with him at our long-time, big-time competitor, the Capital City Club.

Noble said that he had been observing the big picture of racial unrest in our country and particularly in our sister city, Birmingham, where violent confrontations were occurring every day between police led by Chief "Bull" Connor and civil rights demonstrators, and said, "blood was running in the streets." He pointed out that this could hurt us all as well as our entire community. One of my friends at that time was a young salesman for General Electric. His territory included Birmingham and his division was kitchen equipment. At one point, in later months, he told me that the civil rights activity in Birmingham had practically killed his business there.

Ed Noble reminded us we had Atlanta University on our south side, a place filled with black students who would soon be on summer vacation. He noted that we had already witnessed some sit-ins in Atlanta. (I believe that there had been one at Woolworth's soda fountain across from Davison's on Peachtree.) He suggested that we consider the very real possibility that we would ultimately be forced to open our dining facilities.

He said that we should consider discussing that possibility to determine a plan of action that we might better control in our own community, rather than waiting for outsiders to dictate the terms. He made a lot of sense. We broke up, determined to meet again in a few days.

After some reflection, I begged off the second meeting and asked my good friend John Evans to take a message to that meeting. Most of Herren's competition consisted of three downtown private clubs: the Commerce Club, the Athletic Club, and the Capital City Club. In addition to the clubs, there were more in-house executive dining rooms such as the one in the new Bank South building. I felt none of these would ever have to integrate. This evaluation proved all too accurate. I felt we would be committing suicide to join in such a plan.

Then I went home and talked with Beautiful Jane until the

small hours of the morning. As she has always done, she calmly analyzed the situation and suggested we should be a part of the discussions and a participant in whatever was decided. So I rejoined.

Meetings continued every few days, at all hours of the day and night. Ultimately we spent more than 100 hours in these meetings. Toward the end, one lasted until nearly 1:00 A.M. The participants varied. We asked that only owners, not managers, be present. Sometimes we invited members of the black community who had been identified to us as leaders.

The reader has to understand that then, as today, there are no real leaders of any community or group, except the business owners who absolutely speak for themselves and their investment in their own future. The other side, though well intentioned, has no vested interest, nothing at stake, and does not and cannot represent anything other than their own opinion and the opinions of others as expressed to them.

Likewise, our Restaurant Association had no control over the decisions of its members. There was a continuing demand that the Association take a stand. To do so would have probably been illegal, and probably would also have destroyed the Association, all to no avail. It was a decision for each owner.

At this point I met Mike Mescon, who held the Chair of Private Enterprise at Georgia State University. He became a great friend and helped me to retain my sanity through those weeks. We asked him to draft a statement in the name of the Restaurant Association saying the Association could not be involved in this situation. He did a great job. We bought a full page in *The Atlanta Constitution* to display the statement he crafted.

Basically it said that integration was not in the purview of the Restaurant Association but a decision of the individual owners of each business. I received congratulations from many who read "segregation" into those words. Others, reading it correctly, offered sympathy, saying something like, "You've got a tough decision to make."

We had more meetings.

Our discussions seesawed back and forth with everyone given plenty of time to speak. We heard reports from other parts of the country. We heard all manner of rumors. I received a call from Congressman Charles Weltner, whom I knew and admired greatly. He offered to help. I told him that I would convey his thoughts. Though crediting his good intentions, they insisted that they wanted to remain independent of political ties.

There was no leader of the movement. Each meeting we assigned a different chairman. At one point I was seated to the left of the leader. He suggested we should poll the group to determine the general feeling on the issue and called on the man at his right, Joe Daole of Dale's Cellar, whom I always remember as a great and courageous American.

Simply (I paraphrase), Joe said he thought that we should get on with it and start serving everyone, regardless of race. I did not know at the time that he was in the process of adding a branch of his fine restaurant to the Henry Grady Hotel and had invested quite a bit of time, energy, and money. On hearing of his position, the hotel manager, whose segregationist racial views were widely known, summarily threw him out.

As the statements continued down his side of the table, each successive member agreed with him. The sentiment grew stronger as it went around the table, and each succeeding speaker caught the excitement of the moment. Had Joe delivered a resounding diatribe in opposition, I had (and have now) no doubt that there might have been some who would have taken a different position. Had I been asked first, I would probably have dissolved on the spot!

Once a consensus was achieved, it was time to call in others to seek the widest possible base. It also was time to start negotiating with the "other" side to develop a plan. We were introduced to a handsome young man named Dr. Lee R. Shelton, a respected physician in the black community. He brought with him a large silver-framed portrait of his family, a beautiful young wife and two handsome kids. He told us that his wife had no problem buying a mink coat at Davison's but they were refused service at the lunch counter, the water fountain, and rest rooms. He said that, though he could well afford it, the family couldn't just jump in the car and go to the beach; all travel was an ordeal.

At one of the later meetings (which I happened to be chairing) someone had invited our most notorious opponent, Lester Maddox, who owned the Pickrick Restaurant. He arrived in the middle of the meeting, disrupted the proceedings with his very loud and well-known racial views, called on all to support him by walking out of the meeting, and stormed out . . . alone.

As we assembled late one night for what proved to be our last meeting, I recognized a reporter, Ted Simmons of *The Atlanta Constitution*, who was one of my regular guests. He asked if he could join the meeting. I told him I would have to ask the others. I received a resounding *NO*, which I delivered to him. As the meeting neared its end, I reminded the group that the reporter was probably still outside. Someone suggested a spokesman issue a statement for the group. Someone else called for a volunteer. The silence of the Pharaoh's tomb descended on the hall for what seemed like hours, but was in fact at least five minutes. Finally, when I could stand it no longer, I volunteered.

Never volunteer.

"What shall I tell him?" I asked.

"Tell him we have no comment," said someone.

"Tell him that yourself," I answered.

Someone else said, "Tell him whatever you think is right."

And so, assisted by three fellow restaurateurs, Angelo Nikas, John Evans, and one other I can't recall, but with the joint statement attributed only to me, I gave an unprepared statement to the reporter and was quoted in *The Atlanta Constitution* on June 23, 1963 and, subsequently, in many other newspapers and news-magazines around the country and around the world. My phones started to ring, both at the business and at home at all hours of the day and night.

In retrospect, the reader will recognize that, to the general public, Herren's was the only one "capitulating" though there were fifty-five owners represented at that final meeting. Though most honored that commitment, they only did so tacitly, serving those who dared to test them.

The summer of '63 became our time of trial. Even though there were over fifty participants in the Atlanta plan, the others were never publicly identified. We at Herren's caught all the heat from those who disagreed, some of whom have never forgiven me. (Not that there was anything to be forgiven.)

Prior to the publication of that statement, and knowing that the issue was in the air, I received many comments from our guests, one of whom told me, "Ed, I've eaten with *them* all over the world, but if you give in to them I'll never eat with you again." He never did, but many years later, one of his two brothers (who both remained my friends) told me, "All of us owe all of you a debt of gratitude for saving Atlanta."

The next morning I called a meeting of our managers, followed by a meeting with our employees. To my management, I explained what had been happening at these mysterious meetings I had been attending, and said I expected to serve our first black guests that day (actually, it happened a few days later). I asked for and received their pledge of wholehearted cooperation.

To our staff, I made the same comments, adding that I felt this was an inevitable progression in our industry and we would be lead-ing the way. I invited any server to leave without prejudice if they felt they did not wish to participate and added that I expected those who stayed to give our new guests "the same lousy service you've been giving everyone else all these years." No one moved. The only one we lost was on vacation that week and never returned.

Our first black guests turned out to be Dr. Shelton, his wife Delores, and his mother-in-law, Mrs. Alberta Walker. Since my statement had appeared in the paper, all those who objected had stayed away so that there was no stir as I seated them in the front dining room. Dr. Shelton recently recalled that he'd had prime rib that night, and it was the best he'd ever had.

As one might imagine, Jane and I received a great deal of attention from those who disagreed. Some bold individuals even called us at two and three in the morning to give us a bucket of raspberries along with uncomplimentary pronunciations of our family name. Many called to harass us during the day and we received more than our share of illiterate (and unsigned) cards and letters, many of which I still have.

We were picketed by members of the Ku Klux Klan (one even dressed in red). One employee said the man might be the devil himself! I witnessed the delivery of their picket signs by my friend Lester Maddox (who proclaimed great innocence in the whole movement). The signs indicated their belief that I was either a communistic capitalist or a capitalistic communist. One young picketer, said to be Lester's son, developed a great admiration for our hostess and brought her several of his favorite recordings.

This same young lady (she was about five feet two inches) was stopped on the sidewalk by a roughneck ("He looked like he was ten feet tall!") who indicated that it would be unhealthy for her to return to work, a threat she chose to ignore. When I spoke to the Chief of Police about this he advised me that talk was cheap and not actionable. Of course he was correct, but I felt better for the talk, as did my courageous hostess.

The Atlanta Journal, on June 27, 1963, carried a story on page 14 written by Fred Powledge. Headlined "White Pickets Protest Open Restaurants Here," the story told of neatly dressed whites picketing a number of restaurants, carrying neatly printed signs that read, "Do not eat here. The owner of this business is a leader for integration." Several restaurants were mentioned in the article, including Herren's, and the article identified Lester Maddox as "a spokesman for segregationist causes." "There will be a few at first," he was quoted as saying, "but it may run into the thousands before it is terminated."

It continued with, "Mr. Maddox, whose anti-integration sentiments have formed the bases of unsuccessful campaigns for mayor of Atlanta and for lieutenant governor, said he himself would not take part in the picketing.

"He said the information about the demonstration had come to him from 'various groups and individuals' who were opposed to the desegregation plan."

Well, how about that!

At one point I noticed a lady whom I recognized as Mrs. Leike keeping pace with one of the picketers whose picture and sign appeared in the newspapers. She paced up and down with him in the summer heat for almost an hour before he left and she came in for lunch.

She told me how she had explained to this man (a fellow high school language teacher, she at Sandy Springs High School and he from Stone Mountain) that I was a true blue American and a veteran, my son was in the Navy, we had always supported all the good stuff in Atlanta, and a million other things. She said, "Finally he admitted he must be wrong and left!"

For those willing to consider a little humor in even the most bizarre situations there is the following.

I have to presume that all the restaurateurs involved called together their various staffs and told them substantially what I told mine. But no one would admit publicly that they were part of the plan, particularly over the telephone. And the racist opposition was having a field day with the telephones! The people who answered the phones became very cagey.

I heard the following from Angelo Nikas, who owned Camellia Gardens, which was participating quietly. His business was at the top of a hill, and a call came to one of his employees from someone who turned out to be an employee of a restaurant at the bottom of the same hill, less than half a mile away.

Caller: "Are you one of the places serving blacks?"

Answer, from wary previously-insulted employee: "No, we're not."

Caller from the bottom of the hill turned to fellow employees and said, "They're not doing it, so why should we?"

Before I-Day arrived I had quizzed the owner of a neighboring eating establishment who had not participated in the talks. I invited him to join with us. He showed me a sign on his counter and two pads of paper. The sign explained that management wished to know how guests felt about admitting blacks. "You can see how they voted, about 60/40 anti," he said. I asked him what he really expected the outcome to be and told him this was a management decision only he could make. I don't know when or if he joined us, but at that time he stayed out.

Another neighbor, Charlie Leb, was unwittingly drawn into the conflict and became a favorite target of the sit-in kids. He was pictured in *The Atlanta Journal* throwing a young black man out of his restaurant. Lester Maddox was quick to welcome Charlie to his club and encourage his resistance.

Charlie also operated a restaurant in a beautiful new hotel on Peachtree just behind the Biltmore. The hotel was half-owned by a Hollywood star (Doris Day, I believe) and half-owned by the AFL-

CIO. Charlie had the bar and the restaurant. The hotel was scheduled to host a visit to Atlanta by another Hollywood biggie, Harry Belafonte.

The hotel management had reserved the private dining room for Belafonte's group so they would not be eating in the restaurant. Charlie called on me, wanting to ensure that Belafonte's group would find the dining room unavailable. He wanted the members of the Restaurant Association to be sitting at all the tables if Belafonte showed at the door. Needless to say, I discouraged this activity, saying we had our own businesses to tend. Almost crying, Charlie told me, "I'm a Russian Jew restaurant operator—how many more minorities can I belong to?"

Charlie's anger got the better part of his judgment. At one point he put a large sign in his Forsyth Street window stating that the sitters had "urinated in his coffee urns." I heard many of his former customers remark, "I'll never eat there again."

As the weeks passed, participation was ragged. We tried to keep in touch as best we could, but our local problems overwhelmed us. At one point the Atlanta Board of Aldermen was supposed to consider a new public accommodation ordinance. Since I was the only one on record, I decided to attend and speak against this move. Having made the decision, I told everyone I knew that I was going to go, feeling that I would not have the courage to back out. Nevertheless, I did avail myself of a tranquilizer before arriving at City Hall.

As you might imagine, the chamber was packed, and the TV people were there to show and tell all. Though I quailed when called to the podium, my pill didn't fail me. I announced that there were more than fifty of us in all types of restaurants who were voluntarily doing what they were proposing, and the ordinance was not needed. I said that I felt such an ordinance would cause great hardship and danger to those who were not participating and as individual entrepreneurs they should have the right to make that decision.

I pointed out our chief opponent, Lester Maddox, who was there also. Some may remember that he was selling axe handles (I always thought they were really mattock handles) to those who would help keep his business "pure." His opinions were well known, having been printed regularly in the large ads for his restaurant. I believed someone might get killed if he were forced to "race-mix" (his term) his guests. He and many more like him, doing business with many who shared his philosophy, could lose greatly by such a move.

The ordinance failed. Later, Congress passed such a law, but by then everyone but the real die-hards had had the opportunity to see what it was all about.

About that time, a regular guest called me over to his table and congratulated me. He showed me his driver's license, which identified him as "colored," though he did not have the classic African features. I had always thought of him as a foreigner, maybe a Turk.

"I've been a regular guest at the Pickrick for some time," he said. "I never had any problem. But if I had stood up on a chair, quieted the room, and told them what I'm telling you, I really fear for what might have happened to me." When I related the story to someone else, he said, "What the hell was all that stuff about, anyway?"

What, indeed.

We received a very nice letter from one regular guest who said he had to decline eating with us anymore because of our new policy. A mutual friend, my attorney Bob Harland, jokingly said this wonderful, friendly man was so steeped in southern tradition that, "I wouldn't be surprised if he dined at home in his Confederate uniform!" Thanks to our mutual friend who offered to be the reasoning go-between, he returned a few weeks later. Neither of us ever mentioned the letter.

At the time a group met regularly at Herren's, generally in the Gallery at a round table in the middle of the dining room. They were the white element of the Southern Christian Leadership Conference, SCLC, as I remember. Their leader was a Boys' High classmate of mine, Harold Fleming. In the first days after "I-Day," Harold appeared in Herren's lobby at the back of the line with a tall black man whom he introduced as Vernon Jordan, the first black man I ever shook hands with. He was a member of the organization but had refrained from joining them earlier, for obvious reasons. Vernon, with his great affability and infectious humor, became a favorite of Jane and me as well as the staff.

At one point, one of the owners of the *Atlanta Daily World* (Atlanta's black newspaper) started eating with us, frequently with his wife. They were a charming couple. One day, as they were preparing to leave, they noticed it was raining. He commented that they hadn't brought an umbrella but they were parked just across the street. Beautiful Jane, always ready and equipped for all eventualities, took her purse out from underneath the cash stand, opened it to reveal its highly organized interior, and withdrew a slim packet. She offered the distressed wife a folded-up plastic bonnet. The lady, with a decently attractive hairdo, expressed great thanks, commenting, "My hair turns to BBs when it gets wet."

That summer Jane and I were in the dining room at every meal. If anything untoward happened, I didn't want my staff to suffer for our decision. As things turned out, we never had a problem related to integration of the restaurant. Looking back, I wonder what all the hoorah was about. My lawyer had told me 10% would be for us, 10% against us, and the rest couldn't care less.

However, though many wrote to support us and congratulate us, they feared some kind of incident, so they stayed away. One even sent a check, saying he supported us but was unable to join us at that time. We returned the check with many thanks. One lady with beautiful handwriting sent a multi-page congratulatory letter from Paris, where she had read the story in the Paris edition of the *New York Herald Tribune*.

The opposition will be happy to read here for the first time that, though we never publicly admitted it, we took a financial bath that year. They tried to destroy us that summer, but Atlantans came through and supported us for many more years.

It's time to salute all the forward thinking men and women who spent so many hours debating the issue of integrating the restaurants. They met all over town and at all crazy hours trying to reach a consensus. They are all great Atlantans, whose foresight and courage brought our great city through this perilous time. Now, many years later when all the hubbub has passed, here are most of them with the names of their establishments:

Yogi Yohannon	Yohannons Restaurant
Joe Daole	Dale's Cellar
Frank Larson	The Farm
Angelo Nikas	Camellia Gardens
Tommy Biuso	Emile's
John Escoe	Escoe's
John, Herb and Tom Evans	Evans Fine Foods
Paul Anderson	Caruso's on Piedmont
John Stresta	Howard Johnson's, Company
Jack Sherman	Howard Johnson's, Franchise
A.T. "Ted" Davis	Davis Fine Foods
S.R. "Tubby" Davis	Davis Brothers and Johnny Reb's
Tom Ham	Seven Steers
W.J. Holt	Polly Davis'
George Eng	House of Eng
Jess Walton & Howard Christie	S&W Cafeteria
Bill Kramer	Fan and Bill's

A.C. Davenport	Mammy's Shanty
Werner Herman	Riviera
Cal Bradshaw	Four Seasons
Jack Komisarow	Shoney's Big Boy
E.A. Sonny Lewis	Crossroads
Dan Calbos	Cock & Bull
Louis Vargas	Biuso's
Harold Soloff	Coach and Six
T.R. Soldo	Harvest House
Mrs. Eleanor Schwartz	Eleanor's Patio Restaurant
Bob Bradshaw	Bradshaws
Ed Negri	Herren's

Please remember that first meeting at the Capital City Club was called by Ed Noble. He's the guy who came from Oklahoma, bought Joyeuse, that fabulous estate on Peachtree north of Buckhead, and built Lenox Square.

Coincidences

A guest who was dining alone beckoned me to his table one evening and invited me to share some conversation. He told me that his name was Porteous and that he was a native of Scotland. He said that he represented the aircraft engine division of the Rolls-Royce Company and was in Atlanta to visit Lockheed Aircraft Company, having just concluded a visit to their plant in California.

Thinking that all Scots were named Mc-Something, I questioned his Latin sounding name. He explained that the name was related to the Latin word for door and that he was descended from Caesar's legions who had occupied his land some years ago.

Having disposed of this background information, he proceeded to discuss the two large paintings that were hanging in Herren's back dining room. He said he felt very comfortable in our room because ". . . those are paintings of Mt. Slioch overlooking Loch Maree in Scotland." He told me that he lived beside Loch Maree and saw that mountain every day when he was home and frequently enjoyed hiking around the lake.

I told Mr. Porteous I was happy to have this information since people occasionally asked about the paintings. After a while he took his leave and I never saw him again . . . yet.

Several weeks after this conversation, I received an envelope from Mr. Porteous containing several postcards showing almost the identical scenes in our paintings. Along with the cards was a note from Mr. P. telling the rest of the story. He had been enjoying a brew in a pub with several friends after returning home and was telling them about the remarkable coincidence of seeing the paintings of Mt. Slioch. Someone at a nearby table overheard and joined the conversation with, "You must be talking about Herren's Restaurant in Atlanta."

Recently I discovered some pictures in my memory box. One was of my Boys' High friend Rea Eskew, a newspaper executive from South Carolina. Seated at the next table was my friend Andy Robertson, reading his newspaper. Behind the two of them were those two now long-gone paintings of the lake and mountain in Scotland.

Andy Robertson was a wheel in Crawford and Company, a large international firm that is headquartered in Atlanta and was founded only a few blocks from Herren's. Andy frequently dined alone and was an inveterate newspaper reader. With his paper folded over in handy quarters, he would read, not only at his table, but as he walked in and out of the restaurant and down the street. I've seen him on the street in Atlanta numerous times, but never without his paper if he was alone. (Remember now, Andy always reads his folded paper when he's alone.)

In 1961, Jane and I traveled one Friday to Tallahassee, Florida to attend a restaurant association function where I was to receive an award from Florida State University. We had a reservation at the Duvall Hotel, where we arrived during the afternoon and were assigned a room on the fourth floor. Having checked in and freshened up, we decided to go down to the lobby to try to find some of our friends.

When the elevator arrived at our floor and the doors began parting, our first impression was of a mass of humanity. In fact, the elevator was loaded with the Auburn football team, scheduled to play the next day. As the doors opened further we saw that the person in front was Andy, clutching his usual newspaper, with his downcast eyes glued to some story. Lifting his eyes and seeing me standing there with this gorgeous woman by my side (I don't know whether he knew Jane at that time) he raised his arm and, without blinking an eye, pointed his finger at me and said, "Caught you, didn't I?"

In 1968 we were in San Francisco for my very first meeting as a director of the National Restaurant Association. This was an exciting time for Jane and me. We had flown to Los Angeles to visit with friends, rented a car, and driven up the coast to San Francisco, absolutely captivated by everything we saw.

The opening session of the board meeting was held in the grand ballroom of our hotel, the St. Francis. This was an enormous and magnificent room in the opulent style of the early part of our century, with fluted columns and crystal chandeliers. At one end of the room a huge ceiling-to-floor Palladian window overlooked Union Square and a magnificent view of San Francisco. Across the middle of this window was a platform with an intricate wrought iron railing, undoubtedly the bandstand for grand affairs.

In the middle of the room was a U-shaped table with the open end of the U toward the window. Our leaders faced the window while the rest of us were arranged down the sides, facing away from the window when we were paying attention to the business at hand. Since there were over 100 persons in attendance the table was quite extensive. Being a newcomer and unfamiliar with the program, I meekly seated myself at the foot of the table, which put me closer to that window, though still a good fifty feet away.

Though I was tremendously impressed with this illustrious group as well as with the proceedings of the meeting, my eyes would occasionally drift to the window and the view beyond. At one point I was startled to see someone open a door at the right

Ed and Jane at National Restaurant Association meeting in San Francisco.

Guido Negri

Guido inspecting a glass of wine.

Guido and Amalia enjoying a moment at home.

Beautiful Jane

Captain Ed Negri, Georgia Tech R.O.T.C.

Ed and Beautiful Jane on their wedding day.

Ed at flight school.

Herren's Restaurant about 1962.

Wait staff –
mid 1960s

Wait staff – early 1970s

Herren's – mid 1960s

Edna Neely retrieving a lobster for a customer.

HERREN'S
"The Restaurant of the Elite"

84

84 LUCKIE STREET, N.W. (NEXT TO RIALTO THEATER)

★ AIR CONDITIONED

The lobster tank in the lobby.

Real Food in Atl

The **Original Herren's Restaurant**
NEXT TO RIALTO THEATRE
94 Luckie Street   [Ackson 9561

Recommended by DUNCAN HINES

MAY NOT OFFER THE VARIETY OF   HERREN'S IS. HAS BEEN A
THE QUALITY IS THE SAME—   "THE RESTAURA
ONABLE AT ANY PRICE   MEET YOUR FR

THE SUGAR

Main dining room in the 1960s.

Ivan Allen, Jr., Betty Sanders and Lonnie Leonard open Herren's Gallery.

Herren's

Jane Negri in the Gallery.

*New front entry after
1962 renovation.*

Herren's

A T L A N T A

side of the bandstand, walk across and through a door at the other side . . . all the while reading a folded newspaper! It looked like Andy, it walked like Andy, and it acted like Andy. But . . . all this way from home? With the bright light from outside behind him and with my distance from him I couldn't be sure and decided that I was probably mistaken. Anyway, the meeting continued and I put this happening out of my mind.

That evening, Jane and I put on our fancy duds to attend our first big formal Restaurant Association wing-ding. As we stepped onto the elevator I noted that the car was about half full of men plus one stunning blonde. I, of course, paid no attention to the men but was captivated momentarily by the lady who looked me straight in the eye and said, "Hello, Ed!"

Have you ever seen a better situation for the end of a beautiful marriage? Everybody on that elevator realized old dumb me had no clue as to the identity of the lady. All kinds of scenarios raced through my head. Is someone trying to embarrass old straight arrow in front of his wife? How could I forget such a beauty if I had ever known her? Maybe she mistook me for someone else?

Well, never fear, you've probably already figured it out.

All ladies can look at us terrified lumps of humanity and always know exactly what to say and do. She realized my predicament and immediately introduced herself as Mrs. Jim Crawford. I had met her on several occasions as a guest at Herren's and would have recognized her if I could have placed her there. Her husband, who was deceased, was the founder of Andy's company and they were in San Francisco for a meeting. At that point, I looked at the men in the car for the first time and recognized many of them. One *was* my friend Andy, without his paper.

A coincidence that falls into the "small world" category involves a regular guest who worked for a national food service chain. During the six or so years that Beautiful Jane and I traveled around the country for the National Restaurant Association, we must have encountered this gentleman in five or six different airports. But that's not the coincidence. One day he told me he was being transferred from Atlanta. It turned out he lived three doors down and across the street from us . . . and we never knew it!

A lot of people think that restaurateurs are like barbers or bartenders. People want to tell you something that's on their mind, knowing that you can't possibly do anything harmful with it. They reckoned without me writing this book. But then, remember, no names.

One guest, a CPA, showed a lot of idiosyncratic behavior at Herren's. One day he was the last person in the restaurant and called me over for a chat. The chief export of Scotland was much in evidence by this time, so I stood to hear the following quickie. It seems that he had a trusted assistant whom he had begun to mistrust and had decided to replace. To implement his search, he placed a blind ad in the local newspaper (one where you have the applicants reply to a box number at the paper—it protects the boss from someone finding out that there is a change about to occur in the workplace). After about a week he went to the newspaper office to collect the replies. The very first one he opened was from—you guessed it—his trusted employee!

Another late regular always liked the same waitress to serve him. He called me over one day to tell me of a little game he frequently played. This man was not one of those who always ate the same thing (we had plenty of those); rather, he would change from one thing to another and never, or rarely, ordered the same thing twice in succession.

Many people ask the waitress or the hostess or the manager, "What's good today?" He was not one of those. He would ask his regular waitress, "What am I going to eat today?" She was supposed to guess what it was he wanted. As soon as he sat down he would write his choice on the newspaper he invariably carried and fold it over so that no one but him knew what it said.

The point of the story, as he told it to me, was that this lady who had waited on him (she retired from Herren's after twenty-five years' service!) would look at him quizzically and say, "Liver and bacon," or, "Shrimp Arnaud," or maybe, "You look like you might enjoy a sardine platter today." She was right much more than she was wrong! He also added, "I've got to be careful what I think around her!"

Another guest joined us several times a week, though his office was quite far away. It was in an industrial part of the town, and "eating joints" were few and far between. He was in the lumber business and was in telephone communication with people all over the country when long distance was a high-falootin' type of communication.

Almost every time he came in he would call me over to tell me the latest joke, and they were always great. I asked him one day why his jokes were always new. He said he only told me ones he had just heard from his buddy in the Pacific Northwest. "He frequently calls just to tell me the latest West Coast joke."

Even though I had many guests who enjoyed telling me jokes, most of the stories had been rehashed many times, but each was told as if it were the latest thing, which of course it was to the teller. Those were the days before instant communication. I learned to laugh like it was the greatest joke ever told.

One fellow, surely not identified here or anywhere else (his estate might sue), never missed a chance to stop by during the afternoon to tell me the latest. He must have lived in a cocoon because he rarely told one I hadn't heard. Worse than that, he rarely got the punch line right. Not to worry. He was my guest. I knew the punch line anyway. I laughed like crazy! Of course, now that I'm a bit older, they all sound new to me.

Before I forget, I've gotta tell you about the inventive minds of restaurant people. I recently heard the joke about the man who came to the order window, ordered ten of this, twenty-five of that, thirty of the other with cherries on top (you can make this story as specific or long as you wish). The man behind the counter turns and shouts at the cook, "A Number Two!"

Well, that's a little farfetched, but I did hear someone order a "soft boiled egg, well done." And my mind was forever messed up by the waitress who christened our downstairs pantry "the cuss box" because that's where she went to vent about ornery guests or happenings!

In the early days of Herren's we were mainly patronized by businessmen. It wasn't our doing, it just happened that way. One day I was standing at the front, having seated all the guests, when two ladies came into the empty lobby and peered into the front dining room. Seeing only men seated, one of them asked me if we served ladies.

At that time there were "men's grill" establishments around the country, and we were frankly thinking of doing the same with our new downstairs room when it was finished. Had I said we didn't serve women at that time, there would have been no outcry, the two would merely have gone elsewhere. However, I replied, "Oh, no. We also serve ladies. In fact there are two sitting in the back dining room right now." I might even have offered to show them, but I'll never admit to that. They laughed and stayed.

Another silly. At one time we had two waitresses with the same name; call them Alice. Nothing about them was alike, except their name. A guest came in one day and asked for Alice. We had two, but he just knew one, his favorite. I had him go through the entire description of which one he meant before I realized that it didn't make any difference which one he wanted, they were both off that day. I should have let it go by saying, "Alice is off today." Instead I blurted out the truth.

Important People

As you know by now, we served all kinds of people at Herren's. All of our guests were important to me, and I did my best to treat them as such. Governor Ernest Vandiver was standing in line one day and told me that one of the things he admired about Herren's was that we were impartial. I was flattered and told him so, of course, but couldn't keep from telling him that we gave everyone the "same lousy service."

All of us knew how to give priority where appropriate, but the governor had not been seated because all the tables were full. I often managed to seat him ahead of others with a loud statement about "Your party is already here," in order not to upset those already waiting. I'm not sure they were fooled, but I never got called down for this. Governor Vandiver later proclaimed me a "Lieutenant Colonel, Aide de Camp, Governor's Staff." I never knew if this honor carried any special privilege, but I had it framed and it looked great on my office wall.

Not everyone was as patient as this particular governor.

There was a lady who was an infrequent but notable guest (notable not because of her station in life but because her presence was obvious to all the moment she opened the front door). She was imperious in her voice, demeanor, and demands and recognized no authority but herself. She demanded her lunch be served by one particular waitress. (I later recognized that this waitress was the only one who would serve her. Several servers had said, "I'll quit before I'll serve her," a statement usually guaranteed to move you on to your next job opportunity. However, in this case . . . .)

The one who did serve her was known far and wide for having all the good qualities of her profession and none of the bad. Her comment about this particular guest was, "I'll get some practice," which was her attitude even if she served someone she knew would be difficult. She gave them her devoted attention and ignored the bad stuff.

Mrs. X was from a nearby town. She dressed, talked and behaved like a cartoon character best described as "the dowager."

At one point I became aware (because she told everybody who would listen) that she was preparing to celebrate her wedding anniversary. I don't remember which one. Someone who knew her told me all her friends were invited and, because of her social position in her community, many of them would attend, presents and all. The problem was that her husband had been deceased for many years!

She never arrived at Herren's other than in the middle of a busy lunch, when the lobby was full of people, including, maybe, the governor, or the mayor or the president of this or that bank or company . . . all waiting patiently. She would appear at the front of the line and announce, "I'm here." I would write her name on my list, anxious to seat her as quickly as possible because there was no telling what she might say in the lobby. I frequently seated her ahead of others if a table became vacant that was convenient for "her" waitress.

On one occasion I returned to the lobby from seating someone in the back dining room to discover she had arrived and entered the front dining room. She was standing next to a four-seat table where three businessmen were dining, and imperiously demanded to be seated immediately in the empty fourth chair! "I won't bother them," she said. Moving her toward the lobby, I patiently explained that they were having a business meeting and that I would seat her as soon as possible.

I had told Beautiful Jane about her, but she'd never seen the woman until one fateful night. We had attended the opera at the Fabulous Fox Theater and were standing at the corner of Peachtree Street and Ponce de Leon Avenue in a light rain after the performance. This is always a busy intersection and with 4,000 departing opera attendees there were horns honking, police whistles blowing, and traffic was about as snarled as it can get.

As we stood there, Jane pointed to someone out in the middle of this huge intersection saying, "Look at *that.*" A figure out in the middle of traffic was waving an unopened umbrella like the sword of King Arthur and shouting, "Taxi, taxi." Jane had finally discovered the indomitable dowager!

We had another guest who, along with his wife, was nationally known years ago. His company was headquartered nearby and he came to Herren's frequently, almost always by himself. I had great respect for (that means I was afraid of) this man and bowed and scraped before him. He would bypass the line, and the next thing I would know he would be sitting at a just-vacated table for four, one that had not yet been cleared or set up.

It took me a long time before I realized he never ate anything but a bowl of soup. I'm sure he and others considered him a good customer. Maybe he was, if you credit him with adding luster to our dining room with his presence, but not from a financial standpoint. He would order an extra basket of bread and sweet rolls. Using his cane, he would spear a clean napkin from a nearby table, wrap his extra bread in the napkin, and take it with him. I was outraged at this behavior. But he was a big shot.

When our son Steve came to work at the restaurant he noticed this behavior. One day I saw our man storming out of the restaurant.

When asked what happened, Steve (who is six feet four and was in his early twenties) said he told the man he had to wait his turn in line, wait for a two-seat table and he couldn't take the bread home.

I was sure we'd never see him again. Not to fear. Two days later he was back, patiently standing in line and meekly sitting at a small table.

Hooray for Steve!

Unfunny Happenings

There were also a few less-than-happy occasions at Herren's, the kind that they say builds character. Something is nagging me to set down a few of these just to add a little sobriety to my ramblings.

One that comes quickly to mind involves our daughter Ellen, who worked at the restaurant in various capacities. Ellen was walking through the lobby on her way down to the Gallery when a young man, our bookkeeper at that time, who also worked as a cashier in the downstairs lobby, staggered through the front door and fell into her arms saying, "I've been shot!"

He had just arrived from his daily deposit run to the bank, carrying a brown paper bag with the day's petty cash change, about $125. As he unlocked the door, he was approached by a street urchin who tugged on the bag. Meeting resistance, the boy fired one shot from a small caliber pistol in his coat pocket, grabbed the bag, and ran. Our man lived but still carries that slug embedded near his spine.

While this young man was in the hospital we realized we didn't need an extra cashier in the downstairs lobby. Business was slowing down.

Like many things that happened to us over the years, this decline was not sudden. It took us several months to realize that the opening of the Southern Bell Center, just a mile away at North

Avenue and West Peachtree, had gradually lessened the demand for our downstairs dining room.

Southern Bell's new location had a rapid transit station in the basement of the building. At one point I heard Ed Rast, Southern Bell's president, comment that the new building was bringing all their offices together from all over the city. I rode the train out and back once and determined that, once rolling, the MARTA trip took just four minutes from their door to ours. The four-minute train trip put us closer to most of them than they had ever been. We made a concerted, though ultimately unsuccessful, effort to attract those people back to town at lunchtime. We even took ads in their house newsletter to explain the train trip. But they had their own cafeteria, Mary Mac's Tea Room (run by my good friend, Maggie Lupo) was only three short blocks away on Ponce de Leon, and the Varsity was practically in their back yard.

On another occasion, I was standing in the office at the bottom of the stairs to the main floor kitchen when I heard loud and angry voices from upstairs, followed by noise. It was our son Steve, tumbling down as I was rushing upward. I saw a young stranger wearing one of our cooks' jackets running out the back door. I followed him about fifty feet up the alley, where he stopped and challenged me with a ten-foot length of lightweight metal he'd picked up from a trash heap. I barreled into him and was rewarded with several stinging whacks over the head and back. I did manage to wrench the metal away from him (cutting my hand), whereupon he ran out of the alley with me in hot pursuit. I was younger in those days, in better shape, and a little more foolish. I lasted a couple of blocks before I had to give up the chase from sheer exhaustion and return to the restaurant. He stood half a block away, took off the jacket, threw it contemptuously to the ground, and ran around the corner.

Steve had surprised this man at the steam table where he was helping himself to lunch in the unoccupied kitchen. He had simply walked in the unlocked back door, donned one of our cooks' coats hanging nearby, and made himself at home. Upon being discovered and questioned, he rushed Steve, knocking him down the stairs. Both of us suffered cuts and bruises from this unhappy episode.

In my early days at Herren's, we had an employee whose birthday and date of employment were both much earlier than mine. It was his frequent habit to take discarded lettuce leaves home to his rabbits. He always made a big deal of displaying the five-gallon can full of inedible outer lettuce leaves. One day I lifted the can myself, thought it seemed rather heavy, turned out the contents, and found a pile of steaks at the bottom. So much for feeding the bunnies.

Keeping a decent stock of silverware was always a problem for us. I am absolutely positive that we never lost any to normal wear, but there were many ways for stock to become depleted. Some went into the trash, some were ground up with the garbage and some escaped, walking on two legs. Though we counted frequently and tried to stay ahead, we occasionally discovered there was not enough silver to set the tables. When you consider that we operated some 300 days a year, and had 300 places to set to be ready for each meal, you can understand that a shortage quickly became a problem.

Seeing that much of something that everyone needed at home, it's understandable that some persons might feel that we would never miss a piece or two here and there, but just a few pieces a day could quickly mount up

One morning I was told that we had only enough spoons to set the upstairs dining room. We were short 150 spoons since the day before! We made up some of the loss from our back-up stock, and a search was undertaken for the missing ones while I jumped into my car and went to the supply house for more.

That afternoon my major-domo, Johnny Calloway, called me down to the lower lobby where he had surprised a newer employee in street clothes going into the guest rest room. When she knew she had been observed, she scooted up the stairs and out the front door, never to be seen again. In the ladies' powder room we found several packages of silverware, wrapped in napkins and ready to walk.

Though we were not in the take-out business, we did sell our sweet rolls, lemon pie, salad dressings, and a few other food items to-go. Occasionally someone would ask for something unusual like salt shakers or wine glasses or maybe even three cooked shrimp, things for which we had no established price. We would instantly invent a selling price, usually based on what we thought the items cost.

One evening I was asked to price a loaf of our pumpernickel bread. This was in the era of the twenty-five-cent loaf of bread, but our pumpernickel was not ordinary bread—it was baked just for us by Zakas Bakery and delivered early every morning. Anyway, I made the price thirty-five cents, which was probably what we paid for it, and promptly forgot the transaction.

Later that evening I was accosted by a huge gentleman and his wife who were leaving the restaurant. He was somewhat befuddled but showed me an opened penknife with a two-inch blade. He had bought the pumpernickel and, outraged at the usurious price, was going to stick me with his knife in retaliation! His wife, calling him an "old fool," managed to bundle him out the door.

At one time I had bought some very nice little horseradish pots, the ceramic ones with a spoon molded into the top as a dipper. This top sat loosely on the pot and would come off and spill the contents if upset. One of the waitresses told me she was sure a guest had put one of them in his pocket, full of horseradish! I always wondered what that did to his suit.

One anecdote that probably belongs in the area of precautions to the aspiring restaurateur, might be properly entitled, "We Learned Everything The Hard Way." People frequently asked me how we planned our daily purchasing and preparations. The answer is that most of our menu was prepared to order from a constant flow of supplies. For those things prepared in quantity, we based preparation on past sales experience.

Since our pride-and-joy pies were really exceptional, we took guest orders in advance for them from people who wanted whole pies to take home. We tried not to sell from our stock for the day, reserving that for our seated guests. The baker was accustomed to being directed to make extras and was unaware of where they went. We almost always had some left over at the end of the day. Our price list contained take-out prices for our pies, and since we couldn't serve yesterday's pies it contained the additional line, "Leftover pies at half price for our employees."

One day, as I was passing through our bakeshop, I noticed an unusual number of pies on hand. Questioning revealed that there were additional pies to fill the orders of several employees who were taking them home. This had apparently become a regular habit; the pies were not left over, but ordered in advance—not the intent of our policy.

More than once I have noticed a stray scrap of trash under a piece of furniture or in a corner, realizing that it had been missed for several days in our daily cleanup. (This is not meant to disparage our crew; I've noticed this in many places.) But sometimes the cleanup was too good.

We had a beautiful antique sideboard in one of our dining rooms on which we displayed a pair of brass candlesticks. Though we did not light them, we displayed white tapers in them. At one point someone suggested that partially burned candles would give a homier look in our Williamsburg dining room, so we tried it.

Several days later, we realized that the candles were gone. We partially burned two more and installed them. It took several weeks for me to realize that an employee was throwing away the "used" candles!

Orders and Other Fun

Many will remember a time when Herren's was so crowded at lunchtime that both lobbies had standing room only. Then, as now, time was at a premium. Our guests knew it and our employees knew it. Those who were really in a hurry learned how to shave a few minutes off here and there.

One guest told me that he always ate downstairs because it was faster down there. In fact, between noon and 1:30 we frequently served more guests in the less formal Gallery than we did upstairs in the grand dining rooms between 11:30 and 2:00. I always attributed a part of that extra speed to the design of the space. Many necessary items were available from a small service area attached to the lower dining room and the kitchen was closer. Even though that kitchen had an additional duty to provide back-up items for the upstairs kitchen, the waitresses came first. Additionally, the salad/sandwich area was just inside the door.

That same perceptive guest, one of Atlanta's prominent and whiz-bang architects, observed that the more formal upstairs attracted more boss-type guests—older men who could afford a longer and more leisurely meal, and could indulge in a drink or two with impunity. The stairs, even though they were the magic conveyance to the rest rooms in the lower lobby, were not particularly attractive to many.

Bar business was never a high priority at Herren's and that

attitude on our part added a drawback to the Gallery. We had only one bar—a service bar upstairs in the kitchen area. It serviced the lower dining room through a small dumbwaiter, depending on a written order ticket from the server, delivered via the dumbwaiter, with the drink sent down on the same conveyance. Predictably, bar service was slower downstairs and because of that, the servers were less likely to solicit drink orders for seconds.

But one server (you regulars know who she was) was so speedy that one of her guests christened her station "tornado alley," a name known to many of her regulars, of whom she had an army. They played the game by her rules, and loved it, coming back again and again. She had pet names for many of her guests ("old change of life" and "Sweetie Face" come to mind along with "roast beef sandwich" and many others).

When you asked for one of her tables, or were automatically led there because the hostess knew that was where you belonged, she would go dashing by on some gustatorial mission of mercy, glance your way and say, "You're having country fried steak today." You may or may not have agreed, and you'd have to be quick to stop her if you were in the mood for something else, but moments later it was on the table.

The secret of her magic was that she would go through the kitchen door, shout her order to the cook (whether or not he heard it or was even there to hear it) grab the first Country Fried Steak she saw (undoubtedly someone else's order) and be back at the table in nothing flat. Great service for her guests, but someone else probably had to wait longer. If other servers picked up the habit, chaos could reign. Many a cook was blamed for not preparing someone's order (we say "fixing" here in the South) when he never heard her order in the first place.

She had a low check average because she never sold any extras like desserts or drinks, but she sometimes served fifty or more guests in one meal period. And they all loved her. And so, perversely, did we. Nowadays, with all the point-of-sale devices, she would never get away with this. She would place her order on a machine right in the serving area; it would instantly arrive in the kitchen in chronological order, and be printed so all could read it. It would be prepared in turn and the finished product would have the order ticket with it so its owner could claim it, and we would get paid for it. But those were the good old days.

The Fabulous Fox

As Jane and I were going home from a movie at the Fox Theater one night, she really shook me up when she said, "Just think . . . when we started dating in 1939, the Fox Theater was only ten years old!" As we drove along, chatting about the picture *(Here Comes Mr. Jordan)* and the obvious great pleasure everyone derived from their Fox experience, the thought went through my mind that it's amazing how much can happen from one casual or chance event. I have heard or read that empires have fallen because of one remark made at the wrong time or in the wrong place (or even the right time or right place) and I continued to ruminate on the astounding complexity of life and the absolutely incredible multiplicity of waves and effects that proceed from every person's every action.

James Thurber's character Walter Mitty dreamed up marvelous situations for himself to become the hero of the hour, and, of course, we all do that, at least once in awhile. Just about everybody engages in those kinds of fantasies.

Anyway, Jane and I got to talking about the Fox, and the amazing fact that it still stands after the experts said it would fall. The preservation of the Fox Theater could have started in lots of ways if it hadn't started the way it did. It's very difficult to pinpoint the exact moment or event that started the ball rolling, but I'd like to provide my recollections, hoping that you will understand that my memory is imperfect and that I may get a few things out of sequence.

I was awakened one night by my son Steve, who was just coming in from his turn as night manager at Herren's. He wanted to talk about the Fox. It had just occurred to him that the beautiful building was in serious trouble, showing low-grade movies to few people and probably on the verge of closing. Steve had an idea for using the structure: Make an elaborate, entertainment oriented dinner club. In Steve's idea, the orchestra level would be re-floored into several level tiers for dining, using the kitchen areas already in the building underneath. The balcony would be rearranged into seats on every other level with space for order-takers to circulate to sell drinks (balcony for viewers, orchestra for diners). The stage would offer all varieties of entertainment, not to mention use of the organ, The Mighty Mo. We worked till the wee small hours making guestimates of how much, how many and all that sort of stuff. I said, "You're crazy as hell," but he persisted.

Some days later he arrived home with a big roll of extremely dusty plans, awakening me again. "The plans of the Fox Theater!" he announced proudly after my grumpy greeting. Well, I was astounded! We talked more. With the new hotels soon scheduled to be built in downtown and with Atlanta citizens' attachment to the Fox, I was interested but unable to command the necessary dollars to pursue the unique idea.

Then the bomb burst!

Either our soon to be daughter-in-law Tricia Layne or Steve heard that Henry Woodhead had written an article about the Fox and its impending doom. Trish went to the paper and secured a copy of the article. In it, Joe Patten was mentioned as the savior of the Fox organ (with his own personal time and funds). Several days later, Steve asked if I would like to meet Joe Patten. Of course, I was eager to do so and we proceeded forthwith to the empty theater where we did indeed meet the famous man. I believe this was when

Walt Winn was sitting at the console of the organ, playing all the great old songs that I always try to play at home. He invited me to try my hand, and I eagerly accepted. I'm here to tell you that you can't play that instrument by ear. Overhead are bass pipes that you hear only as the sound bounces back from the other side of the stage some 120 feet away. Meanwhile, the upper registers come from the right side of the stage, arriving at the console ahead of the bass notes. The confusion was unimaginable. Walt kept saying, "Play the notes, don't listen to the sounds!" Two minutes of this convinced me that it was beyond me.

Anyway, having met Joe and exchanged a few words, we decided to invite him to Herren's for dinner, where Steve and I might get to know him better, hear more about what was going on, and even tell him about Steve's idea. Well, Joe came (and wouldn't you know that we had a really great business evening at Herren's that night) and Steve and I both were constantly jumping up to do this or that. After the totally unsatisfactory dinner it was decided that Joe would come out to our home on Castleton Drive in Sandy Springs for a meal over the weekend.

During our conversations at home on the weekend, Joe told us about all his communications with ABC Paramount and his relations with theater people in Atlanta. It seemed that he encountered utter frustration on every turn. I became truly concerned for this great landmark that has given all of us such great pleasure over the years.

Wanting to get involved in some way and being particularly impressed with the honesty, sincerity, and utter selflessness of Joe Patten, I determined that I would do what I could to help. I offered the restaurant man's only weapon. I told Joe that we had a private dining room at Herren's and that we would host a banquet for fifty prominent people he could invite in to hear his story and start something going for saving the Fox.

Well, of course, he readily accepted and then said that he didn't know whom to invite (which wasn't true, he just didn't have the right names on the tip of his tongue at the time). Big mouth (me) threw around a few big names as if they were bosom buddies. They were people whose names everyone recognized and who had been guests at Herren's for years, people who called me by my first name and didn't object to my doing the same. I later heard that Tricia had also made some calls.

Well, we had that meeting. And we had some big names. After we had been told that he was tied up and unable to attend, the Honorable Maynard Jackson, Mayor of the City of Atlanta, came. I promptly insulted him by saying that I knew no politician would pass up a free meal. (He was very kind and didn't have me arrested.) The president of the Chamber of Commerce, Brad Curry, was with us (I was on his board at the time) and he was the Executive Vice President of the Trust Company of Georgia. Ed Noble, the financier and developer of Lenox Square, was with us as well as Arnall T. (Pat) Connell, professor of architecture at Georgia Tech and Chairman of the Atlanta Civic Design Commission. Also among the notables was Joe Tanner, Commissioner of the Georgia Department of Natural Resources, in addition to the organizers: Joe Patten, Steve Negri, Tricia Layne (later, Negri), and yours truly. It was a dazzling collection of the mighty of Atlanta.

Trish kept the minutes of the meeting, which I have reproduced here, including the names of all present plus many more volunteers. Also preserved are the comments of many attendees, along with an extensive memorandum regarding the Fox and its history. These words or names do not appear anywhere else. This, hopefully, records the actual beginning of the Save the Fox movement.

FOX THEATER
By Tricia Layne

Henry Woodhead of *The Atlanta Journal* talked with the manager of the Fox, Mike Spiritos, who denied that it would be torn down, but has confirmed to others that it will be. Woodhead says the current emphasis is on its value as an entertainment house and not a movie house.

Joe Patten found the organ at the Fox nearly rotting to pieces ten years ago and has since singlehandedly restored it at his own expense. The Fox is now his biggest love and hobby; he spends a great deal of time there and knows it better probably than anyone in Atlanta from a physical and historical standpoint. His goal is to save the Fox from destruction by having an interested person, group, or corporation purchase it, restore it, and give it to the city as an entertainment supplement to the Civic Center.

Another solution would be to have a public fund drive with donations to save it. According to Mr. Patten, the Fox will be placed on the National Registry of Historical Places on June 24, which is a move to save it from possible destruction, but not a guarantee.

Elizabeth McGregor, an architectural historian with the Georgia Department of Natural Resources, wants it declared an important architectural site, which would mean the federal government could not fund any money toward the destruction of the building. Ms. McGregor is very interested in the Fox from a historical viewpoint and has submitted an eight-page history of the Fox to the government.

The Fox, actually known as Yaarab Temple, Inc., is owned by three theater groups. ABC Southeastern Theaters owns 50% and holds the lease. The other 50% is held equally by Georgia Theaters and Story Theaters. Together they are known as Mosque, Inc. The current lease is up December 31, 1974. Rumor has it that ABC will keep the Fox for two years after that, with the same sort of functions going on, and then after that no one knows for sure.

Mr. Patten guesses the lease to be between $75,000 and $100,000 per year. From the research he has done (which is considerable) he thinks the Fox package would sell for one to one-and-a-quarter million. The building is not the expense itself, but the land is very valuable. The package includes the parking in the rear, and parking near the Howell building, but does not include the Dunk 'n Dine and those other small businesses in the area.

A main MARTA station will be built behind the Fox between North Avenue and Ponce de Leon on West Peachtree. The Fox parking lot will extend from Cypress Street to where the MARTA station is proposed; however, nothing important will be torn down and the property is not close enough to the Fox to be badly affected. Georgia Theaters handles all leasing of the external rooms, such as the Villa Fiorita and Aetna Insurance.

A Mrs. Jackson leases the Egyptian Ballroom inside the Fox and holds dances there on Fridays and Saturdays. Professor Pat Connell of the Dept. of Architecture at Georgia Tech is currently making a feasibility study of the area of the Fox. He is interested in total restoration of the Fox, the Ponce de Leon apartments, and the Georgian Terrace Hotel as a convention center. The area is almost exactly midpoint between Colony Square and Peachtree Center. Professor Connell is also chairman of the Civic Planning Commission.

Others who are interested in the Fox include Charles Walker, who does lighting, scenic work, and designing, and attorney Bob Foreman, with the firm Jones, Byrd and Howell. His son, Bob, Jr., has done a great deal of research on the Fox. Most of his information and pictures are in Mr. Patten's office at the Fox. Mr. Patten said the Fox is deteriorating somewhat due to the abuse it is receiving from the current patrons and faulty management.

Mr. Spiritos apparently doesn't love the building, has

little respect for it, and permits too many degrading things to happen inside. Mr. Patten feels a good new managing director could really straighten things out, as well as keeping the building from deteriorating any further.

The representative from ABC for the Fox is Mr. Russell. Their offices are now located in Doraville. George Ewing, of Ewing Realty, is apparently involved in the sale of the Fox for a past sale. Another rumor is Paramount will occupy the building in 1975.

Julian Harris was a student at Georgia Tech when the Fox was built in 1929 and worked on it as a draftsman. He is apparently still a "Fox Freak."

George Devours' name was mentioned frequently in connection with the Fox, but it is not known at this time what that connection is.

Save the Fox Meeting
July 10, 1974—Herren's Restaurant

Attending were:
Brad Curry: President, Atlanta Chamber of Commerce; Trust Company of Georgia
Ed Noble: Noble Foundation; Developer and Financier
Ann Harralson: Dept. of Tourism and Convention Bureau; sent by Jim Hurst
Elizabeth McGregor: Architectural Historian, Dept. of Natural Resources
Betty Jo Cook: Civic Design Commission
Aubrey Morris: WSB announcer, sent by Elmo Ellis
Dr. William Pressley: President, Atlanta Historical Society
John McCall: Georgia State University, Dept. of Music; wrote letters to National Register
Bill Heering: Former Director, Atlanta Art Center and Symphony
Bob Foreman: Attorney, Jones, Byrd and Howell
Bob Van Camp: Fox Organist; President, local chapter

ATOS
Charles Walker: Lighting and design work at the Fox
Prof. Arnall T. (Pat) Connell: Chairman, Atlanta Civic
    Design Committee
Joe Tanner: Commissioner, Dept. of Natural Resources
Chuck Parrish: Assistant to Joe Tanner
Mr. and Mrs. Dick Fleming: Central Atlanta Progress;
    sent by Dan Sweat
William W. Griffin: Georgia Heritage Trust Fund
Martha Stem: Atlanta Civic Design Commission
Bill Hamilton: Fulton National Bank
Ann Siddons: Public Relations
Lee Dunagen: Georgia Historical Society
Hon. Maynard Jackson: Mayor, City of Atlanta
Sgt. Fred First: Mayor Jackson's guard
Joe Patten
Ed Negri
Steve Negri
Tricia Layne
Bobby Clark: Organist, Greeter
Lois Q. Russell: Greeter

Invited but did not attend:
Norman Shavin: Editor, *Atlanta Magazine*
Gail Talmadge : Political involvement
Mary Gregory Jewett: Director, Georgia Historical
    Commission

PLUS: a list of forty-three prominent Atlantans (one of
whom was President of the American Institute of
Architects) who were not invited and were turned away at
the door, all leaving messages of their desire to help.

In her minutes of the meeting Tricia wrote:
    6:00 P.M. Cocktails
    7:00 P.M. Dinner
    7:30 P.M. Meeting called to order by Ed Negri; made

introductory remarks, welcomed Mayor Maynard Jackson and other honored guests. He introduced Joe Patten who gave a brief history of the Fox Theater, its importance, and his feeling that the theater should be used for other entertainment such as concerts, etc.

Prof. Pat Connell spoke next, giving the importance of the Fox and its surrounding area. He mentioned feasible uses for the area and gave his plan for the development of the four-block area (Peachtree to Juniper; North to Third) for a convention center. Called the area a "historic nucleus" and raised two QUESTIONS: "How can we save the Fox?" and "What are we going to do with it once we have saved it?" Connell spoke of the need to keep architecturally important buildings such as the Peters building, Flatiron Building, and the Fox. He wants to use the Fox as an example of how it can be done. Betty Jo Cook asked Connell about a feasible use plan for the property. Connell spoke in general terms of many adapted use plans, but said he would wait for the mayor to comment on his project.

7:50 P.M. Mayor Maynard Jackson spoke for ten minutes, saying that while he would not like to see the building demolished, he and the city would like for Southern Bell to remain in the city and would not want to discourage them. At present there is a hold on any demolition permit, which must be approved by Jackson, but that he cannot do anything if a court order were taken out for the demolition. He promised to pay a visit to Ed Rast, President of Southern Bell, before the end of the week in order to convince him to save the Fox for the city of Atlanta and to assure him that he (the mayor) will not stand by and see the Fox torn down.

He is very excited by the possibility of the Peachtree North project and said the city would have an answer by Friday (July 12) on the legal standpoint. Connell asked if there were any opportunity for public ownership. Jackson replied that there was not, that it would require public funding of some sort.

Dr. Pressley wants to approach the owners of the building with these proposals.

Brad Curry replied that he had talked to the owners who regarded the Fox as a white elephant. They want a way out and would like to sell it. He mentioned that even the Civic Center is operating in a negative cash flow, so an older building such as the Fox would surely be even more expensive (therefore unfeasible) to operate.

Elizabeth McGregor was introduced next. She gave the importance of the Fox being on the National Registry. It protects it from being demolished by a federally funded project only.

Bill Herring said he was interested in bringing shows back to Atlanta and said the Fox would be better suited to that purpose than the Civic Center.

Ed Noble expressed an interest in the total package price of the property; Steve answered with an estimate of twenty-five dollars per square foot.

Ed Negri suggested we get three or four people in the group to go to ABC to determine if they would sell to an interested civic group.

According to Patten ABC will sell to anyone who offered them what they want.

Betty Jo Cook said that George Ewing of Ewing Realty is the real estate agent handling the property.

Joe Tanner talked to Jule Sugarman of the mayor's office on Friday, July 5. Sugarman said he would put a stop to any demolition permit and would try to talk to ABC-Paramount. Cook wants to sell ABC on the proposed adaptive use plan, persuading them that they stand to make money on such a venture.

Joe Tanner said that with an annual budget of $5 million, there is no way the Heritage Trust Fund could give even $1 million toward the purchase of the Fox. He also wants to approach Southern Bell with buying the Peachtree North project.

It was arranged that Curry, Griffin, and several others accompany Steve to view the proposed Peachtree North project on Wednesday, July 17. Steve then introduced his idea of a dinner theater in the Fox, but indicated that he is now more interested in warding off the demolition permit.

John McCall mentioned that Georgia State University is constantly getting requests for the use of its auditorium for symphonies, etc. He wants to use the Fox for this purpose, also stating that the Met Opera wants a return to the Fox stage.

Martha Stamm suggested calling a special city commission meeting to pass a resolution prohibiting the demolition of any historic important place. Cook disagreed with this, saying it would never work.

Griffin said we need a local organization with the backing of the banks and the financial community such as the one formed in Athens, Ga., with the Athens Hardware building. Seventy people gave $1,000 each to purchase the building, with the banks making the interest. Historic Savannah and other such organizations got their start in this way. He suggested Bob Foreman go to the banks with this proposal. McCall cautioned against getting the owners too quick to sell.

Steve made a statement to the Channel 11 news team concerning the meeting.

Ed Negri adjourned the meeting at 9:30 P.M.

Following in Trish's notes are twenty or so pages of description of the Fox, praises from various publications, and a copy of the application submitted for National Registry.

That's my recollection of how the ball got rolling. Lacking the input from all those influential people the only ball that would have rolled was the wrecking ball. I didn't save the Fox, but I'm proud to have played a part.

Nicole Blackman, Administrative Assistant at the Fox Theater, furnished the following information about the Board of Trustees Atlanta Landmarks, Inc. Atlanta Landmarks, Inc. is not only the Board of Trustees for the Fox Theater, but also the organization that saved the Fox from demolition in 1975. Officially formed in August 1974, Atlanta Landmarks' sole purpose was to save the Fox Theater from destruction. Many of our current board members led Atlanta Landmarks in securing the support and financing necessary to buy the Fox and maintain it through its successful status today. The board currently oversees the capital budgets of the Fox through regular meetings. Board members are representatives and advocates for the Fox Theater, continuing to be the Fox's number one supporters.

Chairman: Arthur L. Montgomery, Retired President of the Atlanta Coca-Cola Bottling Company

President: Alan Thomas

First Vice President: Robert L. Foreman, Jr.

Second Vice President: Beauchamp Carr

Third Vice President: John Busby

Fourth Vice President: Julia Grumbles

Treasurer: Robert E. Minnear

Board Members:
Anne Cox Chambers
Ada Lee Correll
Jere Drummond
Elmo Ellis
John R. Holder
Florence Inman
Charles Lawson
Starr Moore

Eva Morgan
Joseph V. Myers, Jr.
Joe Patten
Carl Patton
Clyde Tuggle
Carolyn Lee Wills
Rodney Mims Cook, *Honorary Member*
Richard O. Flynn, *Honorary Member*
Edward J. Negri, *Honorary Member*
Herman J. Russell, *Honorary Member*
Preston Stevens, *Honorary Member*

All with impressive credentials in Atlanta over the years.

The Wren's Nest

One day, as I was minding my own business, a lady called on the phone and told me that she was Helen Standridge. She went on to say that she and another lady wanted to visit me and talk about the Wren's Nest, the home of author Joel Chandler Harris. When I asked why she had chosen me, she said that my wife and granddaughters had just visited the Wren's Nest and had told them that I saved the Fox.

Of course, Beautiful Jane never said that. During the course of her tour of the house, the tour guide had lamented about the serious lack of money and the desperate financial plight of the owners of the house. I don't know who mentioned the saving of the Fabulous Fox Theater, but Jane probably told someone that I was involved, and they were eager to hear more. I invited the ladies to a late lunch at Herren's.

Joel Chandler Harris was a newspaperman who wrote many books but is mainly remembered as the writer of the Uncle Remus stories, featuring Br'er Rabbit, Br'er Fox, and Br'er Bear. It's believed they are based on stories he was told as a boy down on the farm and are based on African folklore. Mr. Harris, who worked for *The Atlanta Constitution*, had, shortly after the end of the Civil War, written an editorial that seemed an effort to heal the hurts of the recent conflict.

The Wren's Nest was Harris' name for his home because of

his love of animals. He noted that his mailbox was the nesting spot for a family of wrens, who returned year after year. That original wooden mailbox is lovingly preserved in the home.

It was my understanding that the Wren's Nest was owned by an association composed of a dwindling number of devotees, all ladies and many of advancing years. Originally about 100 in number, they were down to something like forty, several living in nursing homes, all individually responsible as part-owners. The income of the building, from tours, was totally inadequate to begin to cover the expenses. A huge gas bill (I believe it was around $700) had just been received and there was no money to pay it. The back stairs were in disrepair, the roof leaked, the wallpaper had deteriorated to the point that it was peeling off the walls, actually hanging in strips in the room reverently preserved as "Mr. Harris' bedroom," and many other things needed attention.

When asked how much money they needed to raise, they didn't know. When asked what specifically needed doing, their answer was, "Everything!"

With no idea that I could do anything about the situation, I invited myself on a tour of the house I barely remembered from a trip when I was in grammar school. When I arrived in West End, then and now a predominantly black neighborhood, the house was even worse than they had depicted it and looked like a hopeless task. To top off the problems, I discovered a reverently displayed Confederate battle flag in the living room, along with an attitude complementing the flag among some, though certainly not all, members.

I read the titles of books on the shelves. One was entitled *How to be Happy Though Married*.

Through talks with these two ladies plus others of the association, I learned that their by-laws directed that the association, formed in the early part of the century, should consist of "100 white ladies." To become a member one must be recommended by a member and approved by all, any prospect could be "blackballed" by just one member. When I arrived on the scene they had voluntarily dropped the "white," but had a stagnant membership.

I was invited to a membership meeting and arrived to find about fifteen ladies present. They introduced me as the speaker! The best I could do was tell them that I would see if there was anything I could do. Then I went to work. During the following weeks I talked with the head of the Atlanta Public Library (I always called it the Carnegie Library) to determine if Mr. Harris was indeed an author of much more than local note. She was a beautiful and cultured lady who told me about her childhood experience of standing outside the library, wishing that she could go inside. Because of her color, she was not even allowed to look at the books!

She assured me that Mr. Harris was most certainly an author of national note and invited me to inspect the children's department of the library. In it, she told me, I would find a wall containing a number of glazed tiles illustrating some of the Uncle Remus stories. She had saved them when the old building was demolished to make way for the new and had re-installed them in a prominent location, the story-telling pit.

I spoke with a prominent attorney about the legal implications of the problem. We discussed the Fox project, which was successful because of the enormous appeal of the property and the active participation of so many of the citizens. I was told, "You've got a tough job that well may be impossible."

Through a mutual friend I reached the head of the West End Businessmen's Association to determine the attitude of the community, which had become predominantly black. I was told that, while the neighbors were not happy with the attitudes of some of the owners of the house, they loved Mr. Harris and his stories. He felt they would be much in favor of retaining the historic home site.

I talked with a number of people about the possibility of raising money for such a project and was told that it would be impossible with the current membership structure. Big money donors would need to see financial and operating statements, by-laws, membership lists, community acceptance statements, and more.

At their insistence, the ladies scheduled a luncheon meeting for about thirty at Herren's and asked me for a progress report. I told them what I had learned and said that they would have to join the modern United States, have an open membership, have their books audited, and start with a clean slate. I had no idea at that time how this was to be accomplished, but they could forget soliciting our local charities with the organization they had. I urged them to consider these matters and let me know if I should proceed further.

Following that meeting, I was told they had elected me the first male member of the group! I also heard by the grapevine that I was working to integrate the organization, and I guess I really was, though the subject had never been mentioned. I felt that my position was to bring the organization into the 20th century and make it available to everyone.

One of the first activities was to audit the books. I prevailed on my CPA, Harris, Kerr, Forster and Company, National Hotel and Restaurant auditors, to volunteer. The appointed auditor traveled from Sandy Springs to West End three or four times (a distance of about twenty miles) before the treasurer managed to show up with the books. I was told that she had made a statement to the effect that she had been treasurer for twenty-seven years and had never been audited! (This same lady, I was told, lived on Forrest Road, named after a Confederate general. When the street name was changed to Ralph McGill Boulevard, after the liberal editor of *The Atlanta Constitution*, she refused to accept mail so addressed.)

Of course the books were in order, but they showed that the organization needed revamping.

A story in the *Constitution* quoted me as saying that the association was organized like a garden club. That's not exactly what I said, but at least one garden club lady who later became a member of the Board of Directors took offense and never let me forget it. The truth was that they were structured as a very small private organization and could not expect support from the usual sources. This had to be changed.

The greatest thing that happened to get us started was that the ladies elected an attractive younger member, Gloria Baker, as president. Mrs. Baker, an educator, was dedicated to doing what was needed to save the house.

Another exciting happening occurred at Herren's. One day a handsome young man introduced himself to me as Mark Riley, a lawyer working with King and Spalding, one of Atlanta's silk stocking law firms. He said that he was interested in volunteering to work on the project and had been told that I was the one to see. Indeed I was! I proposed him for membership, and he was accepted.

Then the president, the handsome young man, and I, along with Helen Standridge and three or four more forward-thinking members, met at my house one night to plan strategy. We decided to abide strictly by the rules and see if we could change the organization. Using the rule that an application for membership must be submitted by a member in good standing, we decided that each of us would propose five new members, hoping that the membership committee would accept them. I told my three kids and two good friends, Ed Smith and Phil Gage, to send a check and do as they were told. They did. All were accepted, as were those proposed by the others.

Next we had our handsome young lawyer draw up a new set of by-laws, suitable for the organization we intended to be. He researched the files of his law firm and produced just what was needed, including a small name change to bring a new identity to the organization.

Our president called a general meeting. Those of the original membership who were able were in attendance, and we made sure that all of our new members were there to support us. We had no idea what sort of fireworks might erupt when we proposed that the old organization be dissolved and replaced with the new one. There should have been a great sigh of relief from the original members who were thereby relieved of the personal liability of the house. There was no dissension from the few original members in attendance. With no dissenting votes and no objection from the floor, we had our new organization.

Through a mutual friend I was put in touch with Professor Richard Dagenhart, a Georgia Tech Professor of Architecture, who was in charge of the graduate architectural students. He agreed to put the restoration of our house up as one of his projects for his students. I don't know how many volunteered but we had to have ended up with the best, Tom Coakley (later associated with Heery & Heery, Architects and Engineers). This young man did a magnificent job of analyzing the house from top to bottom, including the historical aspects. He drew our first plan of attack, which we could use to show to prospective contributors.

To achieve the anticipated rescue of the house, the new board felt that a qualified architect needed to be recruited and put in charge of the project. Under the supervision and direction of our two Tech men, we solicited bids from a number of Atlanta architectural firms.

We gathered one morning in the upstairs room Mr. Harris had built for his study and interviewed a number of prominent Atlanta architects from firms large and small. One, Lane Green, told us that he did only restoration architecture and had been doing so for many years. When asked the size of the firm, he told us we were looking at it. "When someone comes from my firm to crawl under the house and inspect the foundations, you get me," he said. We had found our architect. I found out years later that he was a Tech graduate . . . that made three of us!

The house stands today, completely renovated. It was air conditioned not only for comfort but to protect the priceless mementos of the past. A new cedar shake roof replaced the old fish-scale shingles, which were many layers thick and leaking in many places. The old wallpaper was replaced by new, faithfully reproducing the original paper, which was carefully discovered under many more recent layers. The light switches have been changed to the two-button kind that was used when electricity was first introduced to the house. Gradually the old house has been lovingly restored to what amounts to better-than-new condition.

In 1984, with the new board and the selection of W. Lane Greene as Architect, visitation and public interest began to increase. The Association started publishing a newsletter and membership increased from 75 to 375. Emory University sponsored a course entitled "Uncle Remus Revisited," a security system was donated by Rollins Protective Service, and a professionally trained Executive Director, Madeline L. Reamy, was appointed.

In the interest of historical perspective, there follows a list of officers and directors of the Joel Chandler Harris Association as of 1986, showing, where possible, their affiliation in the business structure of Atlanta.

President: Mark B. Riley, Crow-Terwilliger Company

Vice President: Judy (Mrs. William) Rabel, Community Activist

Treasurer: Gary E. Weld, Peat, Marwick, Mitchell & Co.

Secretary: Ms. Laura Waller

Board of Directors

Mrs. Gloria Baker	Commissioner Michael Lomax
Mrs. Montague L. Boyd, Jr.	Mr. William F. Magbee

Br'er Rabbit, Br'er Fox and Br'er Bear are alive and well in West End.

Recently I had the opportunity to call on Editorial Page Editor Tom Teepen, of *The Atlanta Constitution*, whom I had nominated to the Wren's Nest Board of Directors. He ultimately became the very active president of that group and had just recently relinquished that job. His greeting was, "What are you going to get me involved in this time?"

Strange Sights

Under the proper circumstances you might be reminded of one story or another until your friends get sick of hearing them. The listeners who are subjected to your memory can't escape very gracefully, even if they've heard a story before, but I issue my personal guarantee that you've never heard these before. Nevertheless, you have my permission to skip ahead if you wish.

Before launching into these tales, you must understand that I'm not naming names. Though these stories seem innocent enough to me, the principals or their heirs may not agree. (Maybe it would be better for both if I were given credit for inventing the whole thing, though I do not consider myself an author of fiction.)

A regular lunch guest, a well-known man in his field whom I will call Gus, was a loner. He would arrive late and, as you will see, stay even later, sometimes spending the entire afternoon in our empty dining room. He would read his paper and enjoy a drink or two before lunch. Sometimes he might bend his elbow even more. It was not unusual for him to achieve such great relaxation that he would fall asleep in the middle of his meal. Since he was sitting in a sturdy armchair at a very substantial table, he never fell out of his chair or slid under the table, but would hunker down in the chair, chin on chest in complete relaxation, almost always when everyone else was gone.

On the day in question our dish of the day was barbecued beef ribs (the complete long bone), which could only be really savored by picking them up and gnawing on them. Tasty, but not very delicate. Gus had ordered the special. I was totally unaware of his presence until called to the dining room in mid-afternoon. There slumped Gus, oblivious to the world, with a huge beef bone hanging down from his mouth. Thereafter, I always identified him as "the Walrus!"

Here's another story about another guest whose elbow got him in trouble. One afternoon, when the dining rooms were usually empty, I received an urgent call to the lower lobby. As I approached I could hear that someone was trying to get into the lower dining room (which we called Herren's Gallery or simply the Gallery) and was vigorously shaking the closed and locked double doors.

As I descended the stairs I saw the figure of a man clad in a shirt and tie, garters, socks and shoes and nothing else. The rest of his clothes were draped over one arm as he assaulted the doors. When he noticed me coming he said, "I wanna go to the bathroom." Taking him by the arm, I led him into the men's room, two steps away behind him, and helped him to reassemble his clothing. Even though I had experienced dressing three kids and several grandchildren, somehow dressing an adult is not the same. Especially one who had downed at least one too many and who could barely (what a great word here!) stand.

Well, I managed to get him dressed and back up the stairs. I was a little perplexed as to what to do next. Since I knew the man, I seated him on the sofa, looked up his home telephone number, and placed a call to his wife. Telling her that he was unwell (she certainly knew why, but not from me) and asking for instructions, I was told to send him home and that she would pay the cabbie.

When the taxi arrived, I spoke first to the driver, giving him the address and the message from the wife. Then I returned to the lobby, helped my guest navigate to the cab, and poured him into the back seat. As soon as he was seated, he issued instructions to the driver in a loud and authoritative voice, "Take me to the Ship Ahoy," which won't mean a thing unless I tell you that this was the restaurant and bar on the next corner!

Thinking about all the above, maybe you might like to hear about the guy taking a pill. He was one of a group of engineers who ate lunch with us on a fairly regular basis. This bunch of engineers had worked out what I considered to be a novel way to decide where to eat lunch each day. I think there were ten men in the group, although we usually saw only four or five at a time. I was told that when lunchtime arrived, those who were going out would have a spirited discussion about where to go. Engineers that they were, they first made a list of their favorite places that they passed out to all participants, asking them to rate the places in order of preference. They collected the lists, tabulated the votes, and made a pie chart. The place with the most votes had the largest slice of the pie. Then they affixed a spinning pointer at the center of the pie. As they were leaving the office to go to lunch, someone would flip the spinner and they would go wherever the spinner pointed. In general, they went more often to the place with the largest piece of the pie, the one that most of them preferred.

Their office was not far from Herren's. They would leave at noon and usually arrive about 12:15, when we were usually full with a waiting line in the lobby. I loved to have people waiting, not only because it meant that business was good, but because it gave me the opportunity to sling a little BS or receive a little of the same. I heard a lot of good jokes during these times. These guys were experts at both, and I loved to see them coming.

At some point in this regularly irregular scenario, one of them (I'll call him Fred) started asking for a glass of water "without ice" when he came in the door "to take a pill." Wanting to please my guests, I would rush from the lobby back to the pantry to procure the desired iceless water.

This became a regular occurrence. When I saw them coming across the street with Fred among them, I would make my move for the water so that I was Johnny-on-the-spot when they entered. Boy, did I feel smug! Eventually the time came when Fred stopped taking the pill, and I assumed that he had overcome his illness.

Some weeks later, after several no-pill days, the group arrived in their usual jovial mood, but Fred wasn't with them. While they were waiting for their table and there was a lull in the conversation, one of them asked the others, "Should we tell Ed about Fred?" They discussed the advisability of this suggestion (no doubt missing some sort of pie chart with spinner to assist in the decision). While they talked, I was thinking unsettling things about Fred. Had his illness worsened? Had he died?

Finally, they reached consensus. "You know the pills Fred's been taking, the one you used to provide the iceless water for?" they asked. I had at this point steeled myself for whatever was to come.

"Yes," I replied, "and I hope that you're not getting ready to give me some bad news about him."

This sent them into a paroxysm of laughter. Finally the spokesman regained his composure and said, "Oh no, we just thought that since you had been so nice about scrambling and getting his glass of iceless water you would like to know that Fred was trying to lose weight and has been taking a pill to kill his appetite!"

The rest of them always ate heartily and Fred finally returned, but this story points up two of the truths of the restaurant business:

1. It's good for the restaurant business that very few people manage to stay on any diet, which would mean a complete change in their eating habits forever.
2. Sadly, a meal we don't serve to someone today is missed forever.

Vacation

The following story concerns my friend "Swede." He knows what his real name is and already knows he's going to appear here. Since this is a wonderful story about a great guy and reflects nothing but good stuff, I really should tell you his full name, but I won't. If you know him, you'll recognize him here. If you don't, it doesn't matter.

Lunchtime at Herren's was usually hectic. We had a street level with two dining rooms and a lower level, also containing two rooms, with a grand staircase connecting the two floors in the front lobby. There were days when we served up to 600 guests in about two hours, and I tried to supervise all this and the two kitchens during that time. Our guests saw me running up and down the stairs, making constant rounds of the guests, and leaving through the kitchen doors, where I went up the back stairs to reappear a short time later, repeating the cycle.

We had a regular list of charge account guests, numbering some 500, but we would occasionally have an unidentified stranger turn up in the signed tickets of the day. It was usually someone we knew who was without his wallet or was in a hurry and didn't want to wait in the line at the cashier's stand. One day I received a call from Washington. It was Ralph McGill, our noted newspaper editor. He said that he had been in yesterday, got to talking with someone on the way out, and forgot to pay his bill. He had just put his hand in his pocket and discovered the bill. "I'll be in tomorrow and pay it. I just hope I haven't gotten anyone in trouble." Everybody who walked out with one was not so thoughtful.

At the time in question, Beautiful Jane was in charge of the lower dining room and additionally doubled as bookkeeper or cashier or whatever needed doing. She will attest to this story, though she may not agree on the specific words used.

Swede was a regular guest for many years and always ate down-stairs. I knew him as a guest and always enjoyed speaking with him. He had a delightful Swedish accent and was a great conversational-ist. He is the subject of two stories, the first of which ultimately led to the other. At that time, Mamma still came to work every day, opened the mail and prepared our deposits for transport to the bank. She called me into her office one day and said, "Was Lawrence Welk, Jr. really here yesterday?" She showed me a guest check signed by him, but with no address for billing.

I went looking for the waitress who had served "Lawrence Welk, Jr." only to find out that this was her day off. Several days later, with the occurrence starting to fade in everyone's mind, I looked for her again. At first she could not recall the incident. Since those were the days before servers collected their own checks, and all checks were paid to a cashier, she was unaware that one of hers had been signed. "Could it have been the man you sat down with, the one with the accent?" she asked. I was still in a fog, but Jane caught it immediately. Of course, it was Swede, who had a regular account with us, just having fun.

A few days after this, at the end of one particularly busy lunch, Swede stopped me in the lower lobby, with Jane looking on, put his arm around my shoulder and said, "Ed, old buddy, you're working too hard. You need some time off. I want to tell you what you should do."

With this he proceeded to describe a vacation for us at the Greenbriar Resort in West Virginia. He told me that he had

reserved space for us and included a limousine to pick us up, cocktails in Delta's VIP room, the flight numbers to and from, and other
particulars. As he went up the steps he called back, "Don't forget
your golf shoes and bag."

Jane heard all this and was dying laughing because he sounded
so serious and his proposal was so ludicrous. Later that week she was
processing our accounts receivable charges when she ran across his
account. There were several nominal charges, including the one
purportedly signed by Welk, Jr. In retrospect, I'm glad she's on my
side because of what followed.

"We should do something funny with this," she said, showing
me the Welk ticket and reminding me of his vacation proposal. We
mulled over several diabolical plans and finally decided to make a
spurious bill for the vacation and include it on his account. So we
added, "For vacation as prescribed" in the description column and
invented $5,000 as a nice round number. We sent it off, imagining
the laughs at his office and promptly forgot it in the hustle of other
business.

Some time later, Mamma called me to her office one morning
and asked me if Swede really owed us over five thousand dollars.
Remembering our foolishness, I wondered if someone in his office
had compounded it by issuing a check to cover the bill. I took a
look at the check. Sure enough, there was his company check for
over $5,000.

If we had made the bill for a more reasonable amount, Mamma
might not have asked me and might have routinely banked the
check. I can imagine the bank not paying attention to the signature
and routinely passing it along, and then someone in Swede's office
wondering why the account was short. A close look at the check
showed the signature—I.M. Crazy!

A Restauranteur's Night Out

Entertaining at home is an exciting event that is the culmination of a lot of planning and effort on the part of the hostess and host. In the restaurant business we do it twice every day, and the planning is constant. That's our business, and we love it. Sometimes, so we can get a chance to see our friends once in awhile, we even sit down in our own dining room and become a guest instead of a host. Beautiful Jane thought you might like to hear about this story.

I was frequently asked if I was the son of the very-well-known-in-Atlanta Guido Negri and I was very proud to say "yes." As our sons Steve and Paul were going through their teens, they became musicians and played in various bands. One day I was approached by someone in the lobby who, after ascertaining my name, asked me if I was the father of those two great guitarists, Steve and Paul Negri. Whaddya you have to do to make it on your own?

At the time of this story, Steve was in the Navy and Paul played lead guitar in a band called The Majestics, which was composed of five musicians, two of whom lived in our neighborhood. Barbara and Tom Gallaher contributed Dave, who played trumpet (he's now a professional musician, playing many instruments with his band, "Microwave Dave and the Nukes"). John, the drummer (now Professor Costello), was the son of Joanne and Walter Costello. Two other boys completed the band: Tommy Knox on bass and Curtis Rone on sax.

On the night in question, The Majestics were scheduled to play at the Royal Peacock, the famous nightclub on Auburn Avenue in downtown Atlanta. The featured attraction that night was Billy Stewart, who had arrived in Atlanta sans band but with charts (music). Stewart gave The Majestics his charts. They all read them so well that he followed up by asking them to become his personal band and tour Europe with him. They were thrilled at the invitation but turned him down because they were all in mid-year in college at Georgia State University. Also on the stage that night was Aretha Franklin, early in her career, who brought her band.

The Royal Peacock was the premier black entertainment club in Atlanta at that time, and the job was a feather in The Majestic's cap. Of course, we had to be there for this auspicious occasion, so we planned to have dinner at Herren's with the Gallahers and the Costellos and then go to the club for the performance. I don't remember the dinner but the rest of the evening is still vivid.

Admission was $2 each (remember this later) and entry was up a long flight of stairs to the second-story club. The long tables were arranged perpendicular to the stage, banquet style, and the place was packed. We six parents were the only whites in the place, and you'd have thought that we owned it. People couldn't have been nicer.

As is usual, each instrument had a solo during the show. Curtis was so exciting with his saxophone solo that one man jumped to his feet on several occasions shouting, "That's my man! That's my man!" One number followed the other, each one better than the last. Stewart, who was a major talent at that time, sang his famous interpretation of "Summertime" and had to repeat it several times. We had a thoroughly enjoyable evening and the show seemed short. We were not ready to call it a night.

Dave's father, Tom, suggested that we adults stop by the new-to-Atlanta Playboy Club where he was a member, to have the proverbial nightcap. None of us had ever been to this sexy club and the suggestion was received with great enthusiasm even by the wives.

At that time, the Playboy Club was in its heyday and the sexual overtones made it an exciting place, crowded with all kinds of people and those bunnies. When they arrived in Atlanta, across the street from Herren's, we welcomed them with a huge basket of carrots and a sign in the front window. Blanche Matthews, one of our elderly, rubenesque, super-server Herren's Girls asked me, "When are we going to get our bunny costumes?"

When our wives decided that we had ogled enough, it must have been around 2:00 A.M. We had been indulging more or less since about 7:00 P.M. and were feeling very little pain. As we exited the front door, someone spotted Herren's across the street and said, "Hey, let's have some breakfast." Sounded great to me! One of the privileges of being the owner is having a set of keys to the kingdom.

We entered the darkened restaurant and I led the folks down the grand staircase to Herren's Gallery. (I figured with the doors closed it was more appropriate for the occasion.) The kitchen and food lockers were closer to the dining room, which was more informal, the rest rooms were nearby and, best of all, no one could look in the front window on Luckie Street, see something strange going on, and call the police.

Jane led the girls to the table setting and coffee making department, while I led the boys back to the kitchen to "rustle up the grub." We fumbled around and somehow contrived to cook some reasonably good (seemed absolutely scrumptious at the time) bacon, eggs, and toast and managed to get it plated and served.

By the time we left the restaurant it must have been around 3:30 A.M. We were all relatively clear-headed and in our Buick with me driving. Since Tom and Barbara lived practically in our back yard, our first stop was to be Costello's house to deliver Joanne and Walter. It had been a glorious evening and we rolled down the windows and sang lustily all the way home.

As we turned into their street it was almost 4:00 A.M. and we could see three figures standing at the bottom of the driveway. It was our sons, long home from their job at the Royal Peacock and anxiously awaiting our arrival. We rolled up to the driveway still singing.

"Do you know what time it is?" they demanded, as they surrounded the car. "Where have you been?" "We've been thinking of calling the police!" Where and when have all parents heard (or said) all this? Someone among us, surely not me, had the presence of mind to answer, "Now you know how it feels!"

Remember the $2 cover charge at the Royal Peacock? That and the $1 drinks generated a pile of one-dollar bills for the club. When they were ready to pay the boys a few nights later, they did so in one-dollar bills. The morning after the end of their job I happened to be up at about 5:00 A.M. and looked out the kitchen window. There, under the spotlights in the middle of the turnaround, were Dave and Paul. They were sitting on the ground facing each other and having fun throwing handfuls of one-dollar bills into the air, laughing like crazy as the bills fluttered down around them.

Ah, youth!

Champagne and Other Promotions

Very few businesses can survive in a vacuum. The advertising gurus used to tell us about the big chocolate manufacturer who decided that he was so well known that he didn't need to advertise. As the story goes, his business fell drastically in a short time and he hastily scrambled back on the bandwagon.

Early in my career I was standing in our lobby when a guest asked our cashier to order a cab for him. "It'll probably take half an hour," he complained. "I'll go and get one for you," I volunteered, and set out for the cab stand at the Ansley Hotel. The stand at the side door of the Ansley was on Williams Street, in the same relative position as our front door and one block north of Luckie Street. It took me not more than two minutes to get in the first cab on the stand. "Take me around the corner to Herren's Restaurant; there's one of my guests waiting for you there," I said.

"Where's that?" he asked, despite the fact that because of Atlanta's proliferation of one-way streets it was almost impossible for him to get to the cab stand without going by our front door, a trip he must have made many times every day. So much for our matchbook slogan which said, "Take any cab and say . . . Herren's."

Beautiful Jane was the ultimate arbiter in all our promotional endeavors, but we had professional help as we felt it was needed. The chronology of what follows is not important, so the order here is somewhat random (meaning I don't remember which was when).

One home grown project was our Champagne Promotion where we were heavily bolstered by professional help. The basic idea was to capitalize on our outstanding lunch clientele and try to bring them back for dinner. We decided to give away something as an inducement. We didn't want to do something cheap for us but of questionable value to the recipient, like a plastic pen or wallet with our advertising. We discussed many options and settled on champagne as an appropriate gift from a dinner restaurant. We would use quality domestic (Great Western) champagne and not be miserly in our gift. For two, three or four, we would give a fifth and up to two fifths if there were more than four diners.

We had our agency produce a beautiful printed piece the size of a nice invitation (about 5-by-7 folded). It was printed on cream colored, heavy, deckle-edged (in fuzzy red) quality paper with a fold-out tab the size of a business card. All was presented in a handsome envelope with a red deckle edge on the flap.

The pieces were handed out by me and my manager every day to all guests as they left. They were to tear off the card to keep in their wallet and present at dinner for their champagne. I don't remember how many we had printed but it was in the thousands. Many of our guests received multiples because they were regulars and were handed one every time they went out our doors. We encouraged them to give extras they did not intend to use to their co-workers or friends.

When a lot of people were leaving all at the same time, I was barely able to look up to see who was in front of me. I placed one invitation in a hand and then looked up when the elderly gentleman said to me, "What's this?" "A free bottle of champagne," I answered as the identity of the recipient began to sink in. It was Atlanta's senior Methodist minister, Bishop Candler, who took the occasion to give me a fifteen second mini-sermonette on the evils of alcohol.

One mistake we made was to have them all expire at the same time, rather than over a period of weeks. We didn't realize that it is human nature to wait until the last minute just as something is expiring. Nevertheless, the promotion worked extremely well and our guest counts soared, particularly on Friday and Saturday nights. The last night we served something like 400 guests and worked until 2:00 A.M. The entire staff was exhausted!

Though this promotion brought many guests and increased our gross income, I never could decide if any of that money got to the bottom of the P&L statement. However, though our servers were exhausted at day's end, I'm sure they found financial benefit.

Using the same agency, we did some radio advertising we thought was outstanding to begin with, but later had second thoughts. The one-minute spots started with a bar or two of some well-known classical selection, like Beethoven's Fifth, and were then voiced by Skitch Henderson, a nationally known entertainment figure, who had a particularly mellow and cultured voice. The one-minute spots aired on WSB, Atlanta's most powerful and respected radio station.

After spending a great deal on broadcasting over a lengthy period we had a survey done because these great award-winning quality ads were not bringing any business. The survey told us that we had overshot our market and scared off our potential guests. They perceived us as a very expensive restaurant. At the same time, any sophisticate who might have been attracted was probably disappointed at our homey enterprise. Realizing that we had overshot the mark, we had a similar ad prepared with a different, more uncultured voice dripping with "dese" and "dose." It was very well done and really funny, but we decided it might be insulting and dropped the whole idea.

That's not to say we stopped advertising. To keep any business going and growing you must constantly appear before your public in some form or another. There are so many ways of doing this that the big boys have a department devoted entirely to advertising and promotion. In a small company the owner does everything. He has continuous board meetings while shaving, showering, driving, you name it. When an advertising idea hits him that he thinks is good, he has to hang onto the idea tenaciously. The next person he sees will tell him the price of lettuce just went out of sight, or one of his employees is on the phone from the county hoosegow and needs help, or the air conditioning isn't working. In the midst of all this, he still has to remember and develop his great advertising idea.

One that came from Jack Lenz, our contact and friend at WSB, was to redecorate our lower dining room into an art gallery, displaying art from selected local galleries. Though this was certainly not a novel idea, it wasn't being done in our market at the time. Through Jack and Ruth Kent, an on-air television personality at WSB, we found gallery owner and artist Lonnie Leonard. He was a former Delta Air Lines sales rep who had resigned his job to devote his life to painting and he owned a small art gallery. (Lonnie has become a well-known and much-in-demand artist with a gallery in Palm Beach and his paintings hang in fancy homes all over the country. He, his wife Shirley, and son Steven have become close friends of ours. He even spent many evenings teaching us to paint.)

Lonnie agreed to become our gallery director and as such acted as liaison between Herren's and the local gallery owners. We redecorated our lower dining room, upgraded the lighting to accommodate the art, and we had an attractive lighted sign made to be displayed over the staircase that proclaimed the space to be Herren's Gallery. Once a month the entire collection of paintings and sculptures was changed, carefully collected and hung or positioned by Lonnie.

Under the guidance of our advertising mogul of the moment

and using the advice of a WSB director, I was coaxed into becoming the announcer to let Atlanta know what we were doing. We served dinner in the Gallery on Friday and Saturday nights and we had Evelyn King playing the piano and singing to liven things up a bit. The waitresses dressed in artists' smocks and berets, and Lonnie was on hand with his charming wife Shirley to talk to all about the paintings and other art. For our opening, Mayor Ivan Allen, Jr. did the ribbon cutting honors and many notables in the art world were on hand including the governor's wife, Betty Sanders, a well-known artist in her own right.

Almost every time I entered the Gallery, Evelyn would launch into "Hail to the Chief." In later years, when the Gallery had closed and she was working in another venue, if she noticed Jane and me entering the room she would repeat this. She was a talented artist and muchly appreciated by our guests.

The Gallery was an instant success. People enjoyed the art and even bought some. The artists had another place to display their work besides traditional galleries. In addition, their work was viewed and bought by our multitude of lunch guests all through the week, many of whom had possibly never been to an art gallery. We continued for a number of years, retreating only after our weekend guest count tapered off to the point that all our Friday and Saturday guests could be accommodated in the main dining room.

In 1975, we decided to expand into the Buckhead area and built an intimate restaurant called e.j.'s, which featured lunch, dinner, and midnight breakfast. We used lower case letters for the name and told those who asked that the the e was for me, the j for Jane, the s for Steve and the apostrophe for Tricia. The lunch and dinner were patterned after Herren's and that whole adventure would call for another few hundred pages. The midnight breakfast was under the direction of our jazz-buff son Steve, and featured nationally known jazz performers, a truly unique venue at the time.

With the new restaurant came new promotional challenges. The obvious target was the lunch crowd at Herren's with a cross reference table tent for our downtown out-of-town guests, suggesting that if they liked Herren's but wanted something a little different the next night they might try e.j.'s in Buckhead.

At the same time we had to let other Atlantans know about our new venture. I liked the radio because I felt that it was very personal and that people driving in their cars were almost forced to listen to your spot. In addition, I had become addicted to talk stations and felt that a radio spot on such a station would be heard almost as a continuation of the regular programming, thus giving us a better chance to capture the listener's attention. In addition (in case you haven't already detected it), I like to try to be humorous, even though I know that you can repeat a funny ad too many times.

With all this in mind, I have to tell you my ego and my desire to cut expenses combined to make me the radio voice of the new enterprise. Not only did I voice the spots but I wrote them too, smugly thinking I could tell a better story about our business than some outsider who would simply revert to canned restaurant phrases.

Since our phone rang continuously with people asking where we were, I attempted to direct them on the air as well as in some of our newspaper ads, also done in a humorous vein. The directions were simple enough once people were on Peachtree and steering toward Buckhead. But the tale got stale.

One day I got a brilliant idea and told people how to get to us from Valdosta. "Take I-75 North until you reach the Peachtree/Buckhead exit and then go north on Peachtree to Buckhead and then . . ." followed by the same directions we had been using.

About two weeks after these ads started running on WGST, I received a call from a friend who said, "Ed, I've been following your radio career and like what you're doing. However . . ." (wouldn't you know that the compliments would be followed by something else?)

"However," he said, "you evidently haven't followed your own directions recently. Because of the expansion of the downtown connector, they closed that exit several months ago!"

And another time, when we started serving Sunday brunch, we had a professionally produced ad that used one of the local *big* radio voices (called a god voice in the trade) to suggest that a Sunday jogger might jog on down to e.j.'s for a scrumptious Sunday Brunch. It hadn't run more than one or two times when I received a call from a very prominent religious jurist who gave me a complete run-down on how really insulted he was. I cancelled it over the strong protests of Steve, Jane, the agency and goodness knows who else. It was probably the best thing we had ever done and one of the better spots produced in Atlanta at the time.

By now you know that the little guy basically has to do it himself. Some ideas work and some don't. You may remember some of the ones that didn't . . . I've been trying to forget them.

Outside Activities

A s a newcomer to the food business, with training only in engineering and flying, it became obvious that I had a lot to learn. When Daddy first bought Herren's I was just starting Boys' High School and hoping to go to Georgia Tech. That was in 1938 and a long way from 1947 when I finally threw in the towel and started working full time for the family business.

At that time I put on a white uniform and worked as the steward from my self-built little office in the basement kitchen. The staff, in general, were the people who had worked through the war for Mamma and various managers. I had a lot to learn. I learned from my future brother-in-law Chuck Satterthwaite, a graduate of Cornell University's College of Hotel Administration who had just come to work as our manager, from the help, from the food salesmen who called on us regularly, from reading trade magazines, and from a giant book entitled *Wenzel's Menu Maker*, which disappeared mysteriously from my office much later.

At one point the company owned an antique Ford pickup truck which we parked in the alley behind the store. Every morning I would drive it out to the huge Georgia Farmer's Market south of town on Lee Street, near Fort McPherson, to purchase provisions for the day. (Here we pronounce that *mac-fur'son*. In other parts of the world its *mac-fear-son*.)

My salary was what I had been earning as a second lieutenant in the Army Air Corps: $185 per month plus $50 "hazardous duty pay bonus." We were living with our two boys in a way-out suburb, Chamblee, where our house payments were something like $68 per month, and where our daughter Ellen was born. We had many great young neighbors with scads of children. Some of us men of the house carpooled back and forth to Atlanta when we could. When we were riding along and the topic of "integration and segregation" came up, old stupid me hardly knew what they were talking about. Those were the days when they began building the expressway through town and had finished it only from downtown to the Brookwood Station on Peachtree Road. I learned a lot from those guys, Tom "Woody" Moore and "Pop" Brooks.

Early on I discovered the fairly newly formed Atlanta Restaurant Association and joined. At my first meeting the speaker was John Evans, President of Evans Fine Food. Among other things, he told us he and his two brothers, Tom and Herb, had a chain of three small eating places with a commissary he ran as support for the three restaurants. His early introduction to the food industry was up north with someone like the White Castle chain. He said he had made up his mind that if he had to work in the business he was going to position himself so he would never have to work at night. I liked that!

I became active in the Association and was elected to its presidency in 1959. A couple of activities from that time have stuck with me. During the summer of '59, my board of directors decided to have a grand picnic outing for the entire membership. We reserved an appropriate date at Lake Spivey, an entertainment area south of Atlanta, and notified the membership. The food was to be furnished by all the members of the board of directors, each bringing his specialty. I elected Shrimp Arnaud and managed to get our supplier, Capitol Fish Company, to furnish a 50-pound case of the 21/25 size shrimp we usually bought from them.

Our contribution of the Arnaud Sauce came from a recipe in use when Daddy bought Herren's that had probably been modified by him or the help in the ensuing years. One of the directors owned a cafeteria in the Broadview Plaza out on Piedmont Road and offered to bring 144 dozen deviled eggs! He later commented that he didn't realize what he was offering. "Everybody in the kitchen was working and every flat surface was covered with deviled eggs!" But they were delicious and quickly scarfed up. The event was a smashing success. Many of those who attended were likely not families of members or even members, but most ate like there was no tomorrow and all had a hilarious time.

Another activity was the promotion of mixed drinks in the city. The state had already gone "wet" with a county option provision, and liquor was being sold from stores under state control. The state control of liquor sales dictated the size of advertising in the front window and also directed that there be no back door to the establishment. No doubt the thinking was that activity could be more clearly observed by just one agent. But the fire departments thought otherwise and they always called for two means of exit from all buildings. However, mixed drinks were still prohibited in Atlanta. We could serve beer and wine but not the hard stuff. There were no bars as such that I knew of except a small one in the Ansley Hotel right around the corner from us. Nevertheless some restaurants managed to pour drinks anyway, under a "wine pouring license."

Every once in awhile the word would come down that District Attorney Hinson McAuliffe, (a Boys' High boy in my '40 class) was on the warpath. He was said to have evidence in the form of previously collected samples of mixed drinks from us and many of our competitors and we were cautioned to discontinue serving for a time. Nothing ever came from this activity that I know of, but it scared me.

At one point there was a meeting called at Atlanta Police Headquarters to discuss alcohol sales. The seating arrangement was in the form of an L with bench-type seating in three or four tiers. Our opponents were seated on the bottom of the L and led by two ministers, one of whom was the fiery Louie D. Newton. The other was the pastor of the Morningside Baptist Church. They were accompanied by many members of their flocks. We bad guys were seated along the leg of the L and led by yours truly along with Carling Dinkler, Jr. (owner of the Dinkler Plaza Hotels), Angelo Nikas, (owner of Camellia Gardens), and many other hard-working restaurateurs. We were trying to preserve our business and bring our city into the modern world.

The preachers told numerous stories of anguished wives begging them to intercede with drunken husbands. We grimly countered with the idea that drinking in our establishments would have a degree of control—our drinkers' drinks would be limited while those buying by the bottle and drinking elsewhere might become the subjects of wives' anguished tales. Ultimately the city issued licenses for mixed drinks, and at a large price. Herren's could have had Number 1.

For a time one of our lunchtime regulars was a gentleman representing a British organization with offices in Atlanta. On one election day, when we were not allowed to serve alcohol of any kind until the polls closed, I was called to his table. He told me he was told he could not have his usual drink before lunch and complained loudly but humorously, "But I cahnt even vote!" To preserve foreign relations, I directed that his drink be brought in a teapot and poured in a coffee cup. Maybe the start of Long Island Tea?

Another regular, Sam Massell, who ultimately served ably as mayor of Atlanta, told me he had celebrated his election with dinner at Herren's and a drink before 7:00.

Several years after serving as president of the Atlanta Association I made it to the Presidency of the Georgia Restaurant Association where I served '65–'66. It was my job to travel around the state, meeting with other restaurateurs. At one point it was my pleasure to meet the brothers who were operating The Green Frog on U.S.1 in Waycross, Bill and Denham Darden. While their beautiful and personable wives entertained our ladies, they showed us through the Frog. Included in the tour was a look at their filing cabinets. One amazing four-drawer cabinet was crammed full of instructions that covered every move of every member of their staff. When I-75 opened, bypassing Waycross and U.S.1, these enterprising young men showed up in Florida with those files and a new restaurant they called Red Lobster. The rest is history.

Through my travels in the state I met other young entrepreneurs who joined me in my credit card adventure. In Atlanta the big downtown competing department stores—Rich's, Davison's and J.P. Allen—had issued a joint embossed metal credit card that was honored by each, but billed separately. At that time there were no fine department stores in the suburbs, and all three stores were within walking distance of each other. All shopping was accomplished by riding the trolleys to town, and the sidewalks were crowded with shoppers, particularly on Forsyth Street, just one door away from Herren's on Luckie Street.

We had quite a few guests who indicated they would like to sign their checks and be billed monthly. The idea came to us that we might issue a card to our customers and that it might be made useful at other spots around the state. There were about six of us who agreed to honor each other's special customers who had the card. This was before Diner's Club, American Express, and MasterCard. We had no central billing office. Each user would be billed by the individual restaurant.

With the help of the Addressograph Company, we designed and ordered 5,000 plastic cards with Herren's on the front and the others on the back. Around the state the others did the same, though all did not use plastic cards. (One I remember in particular was The Pirate's House in Savannah, operated by Jim Casey and Herb Traub.) Then we sat down and started trying to name as many of our regular customers as we could. The research for addresses was humbling. Of course, we included some people who were well-known but not necessarily regulars. Among them were Senator Herman Talmadge, who did use the card occasionally, and his personal secretary, Miss O.N. "Dottie" Foster, our personal friend and an occasional guest in our home.

We sent these names and addresses to Addressograph to emboss on our cards and designed a special mailing piece with a window envelope to show the name and address on the card. Shortly after the first mailing an unthought-of problem popped up. One of our regulars was architect Minton Braddy, in charge at one time of the expansion of Atlanta's magnificent Hartsfield International Airport. A customer whom I recognized but whose name I did not know called me down because I had not sent him a card and he sat right next to Minton in the office!

We didn't know all of them, but most of the 5,000 cards were eventually used. We never knew what use the other restaurants made of the cards, but we had a booming credit card business. Keeping books on all this activity and billing at the end of the month was more work than we envisioned. Beautiful Jane and I spent many Sundays in the office just working on the statements. We were finally relieved of this when the C&S Bank issued its credit card along with the very first Bank of America cards. At that time they could simply send them to their customers. With the flood of national cards, we realized we could end up honoring ours for persons who might not qualify for the bank cards and maybe some who might even be poor credit risks.

Taking this opportunity to reduce the enormous office work engendered by the cards, we decided to send one last billing to our regulars. We included a letter urging them to use a national card instead. Even though we had to pay a commission for this service, it came as a great relief to us. What all this activity meant for the business might be debatable, but the business did grow.

In 1967, my friend Ted Davis nominated me to be a director of the National Restaurant Association, a position he had just finished serving. Ted was the other part of the legendary Davis Brothers Restaurants (with brother Tubby) who operated numerous cafeterias in Atlanta and around the state. He met Colonel Sanders, who was also a board member of the National Restaurant Association, and as I remember it, Sanders insisted that Davis take the franchise for his Kentucky Fried Chicken establishments for a large portion of the southeast. Eventually, I believe Ted owned some 165 KFCs.

Service on that board was quite an experience. The job entailed meetings all over the country, always dining in the finest establishments while rubbing elbows with the leaders in the restaurant industry. At one meeting I was privileged to introduce the new International House of Pancakes to the audience. A committee I served on developed the "We're Glad You're Here" slogan. Some will remember that it was emblazoned on the convertible carrying the mayor of Chicago and the astronauts just returned from the moon in 1969. It is still used by restaurants all over the country in many imaginative ways.

One day I was sitting in a meeting next to Dick Brennan, of the famous Brennan's of New Orleans. His company had just opened a new endeavor in Biloxi, Mississippi, when it was swept away by a hurricane. I was commiserating with him because I knew that they had been remodeling an old mansion behind our e.j.'s in Buckhead, when a machine accidentally pulled the natural gas line out of the ground and disconnected it from the meter in the house. The resulting explosion completely destroyed the house. He informed me that they had also been remodeling a mansion in Houston, I think, when they had a similar experience with the old walls. Boy! Sometimes it doesn't pay to get up in the morning.

One meeting of the Directors of the National Restaurant Association was held in Kansas City, where we arrived by air in the middle of a snowstorm. When we were finally ensconced in our hotel, we joined many members of the board in the suite occupied by our president. This happened to be The Presidential Suite, a favorite of President Harry Truman in his day. It even had a grand piano!

As at all the meetings, there were all kinds of separate entertainment for our ladies, most of which Beautiful Jane attended. At one she heard a story from the wife of past president Jud Putsch (1963), who owned Putsch's Restaurants in Kansas City. She cogitated on the information she received and came up with a limerick about what she had heard. Our friend, GM exec Herb Davenport, was an expert at writing Olde English script. We prevailed on him to enshrine Jane's limerick in that style, which he did expertly. Then she had it beautifully framed.

As she heard it, during Jud's term as President of NRA he had traveled to Limerick, Ireland, where he was feted by the mayor and other dignitaries of that city. Sometime after his return to the United States he received a call from Limerick's mayor. Presumably the mayor asked for some financial assistance. At the formal dinner that year, I wanted her to read her composition to the assembled crowd. When she demurred, big mouth me managed to get put on the program to make a few comments.

I called Jud to the podium and made reference to Jud's experience. That was followed by the reading of this lyric and which I presented to him. I hope he still has it on the wall of his office.

There once was a mayor of Limerick
Who called 'cross the sea with a gimmerick
Asked Jud for a wad
Said Jud, "By God,
I feel that my wallet's too slimmerick."

I know, even though she'll never admit it, that Jane was the darling of the evening.

In late 1972, the board called for volunteers to participate in the Hennessey Award promotion. Not knowing nearly enough and thinking I would be one of the many, I volunteered, and was probably the only one! Named in honor of John L. Hennessy, who helped organize the Food Service Program for the Air Force, there were to be two awards: one to the best enlisted men's dining room at small bases, and one for the huge, frequently multiple facilities at large bases. The facilities to be judged were determined by the Air Force, one in each command around the world!

I was chosen (from a group of one?) to be on the team judging the single facility dining rooms. It would entail something like a three-week trip around the world. Wow! My team consisted of Bob Horn, Director of Food Service at the Kodak Company in Rochester, New York, Air Force Captain Craig DeMoss, who was to be our guide, and me. Bob and I were issued regular Air Force orders to make the trip and designated brigadier generals for the duration. We met on March 6, 1973 at Andrews Air Force Base. We were escorted through a huge waiting room, peopled by military personnel and their families and baggage, to a small waiting room in back. Here we found a ticket desk with a uniformed ticket agent.

Captain DeMoss approached the agent and produced his orders and ours. Then he left the room, telling us that he did not have enough rank to be in the room! We noted an Army colonel and his wife and a Navy admiral and his wife. Outside we saw a jet on the tarmac with boarding stairs in place. An Air Force blue staff car appeared at the door and the admiral and his wife boarded for the two-second ride to the aircraft. The car returned for the colonel and his wife, who were also driven to the plane. When the car returned, we were told it was for us. We declined and walked.

When we were seated we noted a long line of enlisted personnel and their families coming toward the plane, led by Captain DeMoss. Seated three abreast on both sides of the aisle, we were in the first rank on the left with a seat between us for DeMoss. The admiral and his wife were seated across from us with his hat between them with all its golden scrambled eggs on the bill. After the door was closed, the flight attendant came to the front and asked if that middle seat was taken because she had one traveler who had no seat. The admiral removed his hat and an Air Force sergeant took the seat. As soon as we were airborne the sergeant left the seat between the admiral and his wife and never returned. We never knew where he spent the flight.

We had embarked on a huge (for the times) jet for Torrejon Air Force Base near Madrid, Spain, for a beautiful flight through the night and into the dawn as we crossed the Spanish coast. As we taxied to the parking spot at the air base, we saw a welcoming committee with a company of airmen, a color guard, and a band, led by the base commander who, I believe, was enjoying his first day as a brigadier general. Our gold-braided admiral sitting across the aisle from us was getting spiffed up for his arrival. He, like us, probably assumed the welcoming committee was for him. We assumed we would follow him and his beautiful wife down the stairs.

Imagine everyone's surprise when the cabin door opened and an airman entered to announce in a loud voice. "The Hennessey Committee will deplane first . . . who's that?"

Ahem!

Our job was to evaluate the enlisted men's dining room at this fighter base. Captain DeMoss cautioned us that it would be a super great facility, as would all the succeeding bases. He cautioned us to reserve the very top grades until we had seen them all; no matter how good these men were, we still might see some better. And he was absolutely correct.

We were installed in the quarters reserved for visiting dignitaries and given the royal treatment. I remember being told that the most recent occupant of Bob's room was Marilyn Monroe. We spent plenty of time checking the kitchen, receiving, storage, and dining areas, and our visit included sitting down and eating several meals with the airmen. Our first agreement was that these men serving our country were surely well-treated and may have had the best job of their lives.

While we were on the base, Colonel Johnson squired us around. To a degree we were tourists and the good colonel made sure we saw all the sights. Included were the Queen's Palace (about six blocks square) and The Valley of the Dead, with its 700-foot cross on top of a mountain containing a cavern with a basilica in the exact center under the cross. We were in El Greco's home town where I tried out my high school and college Spanish. (I'm sure I was understood, but I didn't understand the rapid-fire answer.) And our tour of Madrid during the day and night was absolutely splendiferous. One night we had a sumptuous meal at La Puerta de Moros with its palatial atmosphere. Then it was on to the next base.

We boarded a flight out of Madrid, went through customs in New York, and then on to Richards-Gebaur AFB near Kansas City. I remember being told that it was mainly a communications facility with little flying activity—more visiting dignitary's accommodations and royal treatment. Then on to Dyess AFB, a SAC base near Abilene, Texas. All the big birds were away from the field on a mission while we were there, but we enjoyed the stay and learned that one should always pass both the salt and pepper at the same time in one hand.

Leaving Dyess, we were taken to the airport in a staff car and found a big Air Force twin-engine plane awaiting our departure with one-star flags at the bottom of the stairway and a one-star flag on a small staff sticking out of the pilot's window (for us generals, dontcha know). We were the only passengers on the flight to the

Air Force Academy, who are contestants every year because they are the only facility in that command.

Though it was springtime, we awakened the first morning to snow on the ground and deer roaming the grounds. I was summoned to the office of the commandant, Lieutenant General Clark, I believe. Apparently he was a West Point classmate of my good friend Colonel Phil Gage, USA Ret., who had called him to mention my name. He welcomed me in his huge office overlooking the magnificent campus, and I left feeling like something special.

From there we flew to Seattle, where we boarded a commercial plane bound for Taipei, Taiwan, to investigate two facilities. The first leg of the flight included an overnight stop in Tokyo where we were driven down the main street to our hotel past a restaurant which I am positive was called Benihana of New York! We had Kobe beef steaks for dinner in the magnificent dining room at the hotel and enjoyed the music of a young man playing a grand piano. We were cautioned not to tip the musician. The mysterious East!

In Taipei we were to inspect the Taipei Air Force Base, the headquarters for the Air Force in that part of the world. The lieutenant general in charge was empowered to tell his pilots to shoot! We were taken to meet the general who, after welcoming us, commanded our guide (a colonel, no less) to be sure we got a haircut.

Even though we didn't need them, it had to be done. The barbershop had three beautiful Chinese girls cutting hair—two at regular barbers' chairs and one in a private room, which Bob volunteered to try.

What an experience! We had been told to assent to all the services offered: "You want haircut? You want shave?"—even to the shoeshine. When we had enjoyed the best we had ever experienced and wanted to take the girls back home, we were directed to the cashier, an elderly bearded Chinese man in front of a tiny cast iron NCR cash register, one which only registered to $9.99.

He asked, "You have haircut? You have shave?" and so on through the whole list of services, pushing the buttons on the register with each reply, with the numbers popping up and the register going ding-ding. Finally he put out his hand and said, "Sixty-five cents, please."

We spent the required time inspecting the kitchen and dining room, eating with the men and discussing their opinions of the food and service. And we managed to see some of the city, including a huge (fifteen- to twenty-story) hotel under construction with the curving wings at each corner. The building was surrounded by scaffolding made from huge bamboo logs lashed together (which, we were told, had been blown away several times by storms). We ate Mongolian barbecue in a small restaurant where we also experienced beer in various types of bottles (re-used?) with corks instead of metal caps. The garden on a nearby hillside was a view to behold and showed us what the color Chinese red really looks like.

By bus we were then taken to Shu Lin Kou base in the northern tip of the island, where there was no airfield. We were told that it was a post for listening to Russian radio transmissions from across the ocean. This was our last base to inspect and Captain DeMoss' advice about grading really came in handy, for even though we had seen some sterling facilities, this base was the best of all. We gave them the award and greeted the whole staff a few weeks later in Chicago where they were brought for the presentation ceremony.

Our tour ended and we embarked on a 747 for our return to the good old USA with a stop through Seattle for inspection by customs officials. DeMoss and I breezed through customs but had to wait interminably for Bob to join us.

Taking advantage of the opportunity to shop in the Orient, I had bought two magnificent Oriental brass lamps with shades, which were to be shipped to Atlanta. Bob had bought a quantity of yags (phony diamonds). His first inspector said they were diamonds and would not pass them. That inspector called another member of the staff over for an opinion. Bob kept insisting they were "phony diamonds," and they equally insisted the opposite. Finally the inspectors called their boss down from his office. He took one look and said, "Oh for goodness' sake, those are yags . . . let him pass."

This palaver delayed us for several hours, but we managed to board our continuing flight to Chicago and then on to Atlanta. It had been an exhausting trip (was it two or three days?). I was greeted by Beautiful Jane, who drove me home in my groggy state. Taking my bag back to the bedroom to unpack, I found my pajamas lovingly displayed on the bed with general's stars on the collar, courtesy of my old friend Phil Gage.

What an experience!

One more duty awaited me—I was expected to report on it at the annual meeting of the NRA in Chicago. They told me I was to assemble my photographic slides covering the whole trip and concoct a talk to go along with them. They would have a professional projectionist on hand in the banquet hall.

Jane and I spent hours sorting through the multitude of slides and then composing a talk to go with them. After many rehearsals, I was still quaking at the thought of appearing before all those people. When the time came and I was called to the podium I found myself standing in front of a table of dignitaries and directly in front of the U.S. Air Force Chief of Staff. Remembering my days in the old Army Air Corps, I turned and made some smart aleck statement to this kind gentleman as the lights went down.

The projectionist did a magnificent job of following my script. Fortunately, everyone laughed at the right places and applauded when it was finished.

I had completed my six years on the board.

Boys' High School

Over my years at Herren's I recognized a few guests as old friends from my high school days. One of these was Arnold "Honey" Almand . . . in later life called "Arnie." "Honey" came from a counselor in Boy Scout Camp, Bert Adams, whose favorite candy of the day was the Honey Almond Bar. He said, "I can't call you Arnold, I'm gonna call you Honey." The name stuck. Honey played football for Boys' High under that name in '37, '38, and '39 and is still known by that name to his friends. When talking with him on the phone in front of other people, we have to be careful to tell them Honey's identity.

Honey was an occasional guest, frequently in the company of his boss, who I believe represented the U.S. Chamber of Commerce in our town and had an office nearby. One day he called and reminded me of how "we used to run around the school shouting 'Boys' High forever,'" though I didn't remember that. He continued, saying, "We should have a Class of '40 reunion."

That's how it got started. We met several times along with Tom Norman, Tracy O'Neal, and Melvin "Duck" Conger, another football great, all of our class of 1940. We split up the class list and started looking for addresses and phone numbers. The effort resulted in a meeting of about seventy-five at Herren's. Embarrassed to have anyone feel I was making money off the meeting, I charged our banquet price less a couple of bucks and sold drinks from an open bar at about half our usual price.

Someone in that large group sidled up to me during the crush and said in a low voice, "I'll bet you're making a bundle on this." Well, it was a lot of work and a lot of fun. However, when we had another meeting of that group in another year, you'd better know that it was at another establishment, a now-long-gone motel at the corner of Tenth Street and the Downtown Connector. When Honey called me and suggested a third meeting, I told him I was just not up to all that work, and then went home and thought about it.

Honey had pointed out a letter to the editor in *Atlanta Magazine* from a graduate of BHS, who had gone off to war after graduation. While he was gone his family had moved to North Carolina. So when he came home, home was no longer in Atlanta. "How can I find some of my old schoolmates?" he asked the editor.

Boys' High was founded in 1872 as Atlanta's first public high school. It first opened at the James Building, at 54 Whitehall Street on February 1 with ninety-eight pupils, and shared the building with Girls' High. In 1874 it moved to a building on Ivy Street, just off Edgewood. In 1883 it operated for one year in the old City Hall, now the site of the Georgia State Capitol. The year of 1884 saw the boys back in the Girls' High building at Washington and Mitchell Streets. 1888 saw a move to a building on Washington Street followed in 1892 by a move to Edgewood Avenue and Porter Streets, the Atlanta Medical College site. In 1896 it moved to a new building at Gilmer and Courtland Streets with 394 students and thirty graduates that year. In 1909, Boys' High's technological department was separated to form Tech High School, still in the same building. In September 1924, Boy's High and Tech High were moved to a location near Piedmont Park. Girls' High School was on the other end of town near Grant Park (named after a railroad magnate, not the Union general).

Because the new building was not large enough for both

schools, some WWI training barracks were moved from Chamblee, some for each school, where they remained for the rest of the school's history. Each "portable" contained two classrooms; each was heated with a cast iron pot-bellied stove. What boy doesn't remember those stoves, sometimes so cherry-red hot that you couldn't sit anywhere near them. At other times, on very cold days, you couldn't get warm standing right next to one.

Air conditioning in schools hadn't even been thought of. The occasional, surreptitious addition of a handful of rubber bands to the top of a red hot stove would make such a stink! Students would immediately exit through any handy opening, including the windows!

In 1947, the city decided to abandon the separation of the sexes and combine the boys' and girls' schools. The boys' school became Grady High School, minus the portables but plus girls. The building, it was later noted, carried a plaque installed in 1924, naming it Henry Grady High School.

In late '82, it seemed it might be a good idea to do a whole school reunion and involve a lot of others in the work. I'm grateful that Jane went along with all this foolishness and allowed me to invite twenty-two guys from different graduation years to our house to discuss the idea. All showed up on time, savaged Jane's wonderful hors d'oeuvres, and then sat around to hear what I had to say. The idea went over well. They talked back and forth and congratulated me on the great idea, and all agreed "Don't make me the chairman."

Well . . .

During the last week of 1982, when lunch business at Herren's would be predictably slow, I invited three friends to lunch. Tom Norman and Honey Almand of my class plus A.B. Padgett of the Great Boys' High Class of 1931 (as he had named a couple of meetings held at Herren's). I knew him as a mover and shaker and a super great guy. Anytime anyone had an idea for a new civic undertaking in Atlanta, someone was bound to ask, "Have you talked to A.B. Padgett about this?"

We had lunch and talked. A.B. reminded us of the annual award made to an outstanding teacher in the Atlanta school system, which was funded from money collected at a Boys' High meeting in 1960 at the Biltmore Hotel. The gathering was a salute to H.O. "Bulldog" Smith, the beloved (now, but feared then) and honored Boys' High principal. Some of the money was placed with the Atlanta Community Foundation, which was founded by A.B. when he was Vice President for Community Affairs at Trust Company of Georgia.

With the cooperation of the Board of Education, the money was used to make a monetary award to an outstanding Atlanta teacher each year in recognition of the outstanding quality of Boys' High teachers. A.B. suggested that we have a get-together and establish a scholarship fund in the name of Boys' High. "When we're all gone," he suggested, "the memory of this excellent school will live on." It sounded like a great reason and I finally volunteered, "I'll be the chairman. But I want to be like Chairman Joe Stalin. You guys help, but don't tell me no or hold me back."

Never volunteer.

The four of us agreed to meet at the Atlanta History Center and discuss all this with Franklin Garrett, who was a Tech High graduate from 1924. (Tech High shared our Boys' High building and was our biggest football rival.) Franklin was the archivist at the center and a genuinely interesting character. During his early years he was reputed to have ridden his bicycle through all of Atlanta's cemeteries, reading headstones and making notes, and had accumulated an incredible amount of intelligence about the old days of Atlanta. "Stump Franklin" meetings at the History Center were heavily attended. Audience members could ask questions about old Atlanta. Franklin almost always knew the answer and furnished many other details!

Franklin Garrett told us that the History Center had a collection of all the Boys' High annuals, *The Alciphronian*, which we were welcome to study but not remove. The four of us sat around a library table with stacks of these books, passing them amongst us trying to identify someone in each class that we knew to be still living and in Atlanta. The books ranged from the late 1920s to the end of the school in 1947. We managed to identify about twenty-five whom we tagged as possible class chairmen. We even managed to identify graduates from the first two classes at Grady who had been with us for one or two years (we called them '48 and '49, though of course they did not actually graduate from Boys' High). We invited them to a subsequent meeting at the History Center.

I called the Atlanta Board of Education and was put in touch with their historian, Walter S. Bell, another Tech High graduate, this one from the class of 1924. He furnished copies of the graduation programs of the classes we expected to be represented at the meeting. We expected twenty-five or thirty but were stunned to find fifty to sixty graduates who were wildly interested in working on the idea. The lists were passed out to the identified class chairmen who were asked to assemble a committee of their classmates, go through the lists to find all our boys, and produce a 3-by-5 card for each graduate with addresses, zip codes, and telephone numbers. Using my trusty new computer I wrote a letter to be sent to each boy, asking for pertinent information about what he had been doing and asking for his wife's maiden name if she attended an Atlanta high school. (We realized the girls had "disappeared" when they married and changed their names. We thought we could come up with a directory of maiden names with a cross reference to our boys, making it easier for them to find each other.)

I'll never tell who (even if I remember), but one boy said his wife's maiden name was "Sally" and another said his wife graduated from a school in Denver! The answers poured in and, I believe, are still in the possession of Tom Norman, my vice president (now our second ex-president and V.P. in Charge of Records). Tom and Miss Margaret have done an incredible job of assembling, coordinating, and storing all this material over the years. To facilitate contact, I found a telephone answering service in nearby suburban Smyrna that advertised that it was computerized (a new service at the time). They provided me with a number operators would answer as "Boys' High Alumni Association" and record any information they received. I found that their computer "expert" could rarely answer my questions without advice received from the computer supplier, but they collected lots of information. Then I asked my friend Celestine Sibley, the *Atlanta Constitution* columnist, to write a story about us and mention that telephone number. For months afterward, she said, that column resulted in a flood of calls from other school organizations asking for help.

The telephones started ringing! And the calls came from all over the country—one even from overseas! Celestine's column had been seen all over the country or had been mailed by some boy to his friend or family member living elsewhere. Boys were giving information about themselves and mentioning other boys they thought might be among the missing. One boy, not missing in the first place (he was a regular at Herren's), was identified at four different addresses!

We had been joined by Bob Watson, '44, known for the "Platter Party" he hosted as a disk jockey on radio station WSB. Now a banker, he volunteered to be our treasurer. He and his wife Dot did yeoman duty in this capacity over the years. During those early months, Dot helped scour the list from the answering service to find errors and duplications. With the return of all these cards from the class chairmen, we picked a date for a reunion to be held at Grady High School, our renamed-in-1947 school, arranged with the city by A.B. Padgett, of course.

We met on May 13, 1983, some thirty-six years after the last class graduated. We were accorded every courtesy by the Board of Education and had the use of the old Tech High Cafeteria (our portable one being long gone) and the gym. Because we were on city property, no alcohol was permitted.

For the first meeting, having no idea how many might show up, I hired a barbecue catering establishment from south Atlanta to furnish the food. We integrated the nominal price into a dues structure and invited one and all. We rented a huge tent to cover an area where we placed tables with class numbers on poles as meeting spots for boys who had not seen each other for many years. Trish and Steve were on hand to issue the nametags for those who had made reservations and to make tags for the many who came unannounced. Among those on the stage in the gym that evening was Atlanta's Mayor Andrew Young, Secretary of State Dean Rusk, still-with-us BHS Professor Paul Farmer, Tom Norman, A.B. Padgett, and me. About 1,200 showed up! Dean Rusk, a member of the class of 1925, declined to make an address but agreed to say "a few words." Among the things he said was, "This must have been a funny-looking school. I've been wandering around through the crowd and keep seeing old fellows slap each other on the back and exclaim, 'you haven't changed a bit!'" This brought down the house, which was full of white hair and bald pates.

At one point, Tom called on Professor Farmer, who donned a black robe and mortar board and approached me. He produced similar garb for me and took me to the podium where, with congratulatory and salutatory words he awarded me my diploma. I did not graduate with the class of 1940 because of a difficulty with an English class. Phil Maffet, a big wheel in a Dalton, Georgia, carpet factory had his art department reproduce a diploma for me!

We met every year for several years, then changed to every

other year, the even-numbered ones. The organizing work was mostly done by Ed Smith, '40, John Cox, '41, Tom Norman, '40, Bob Watson, '44, A.B. Padgett, '31, Phil Maffett, '41, and I'm sure there are others I can't remember. The Association has continued biennial meetings where old friends from all over the country get to meet and greet. Also continued is the annual awarding of scholarships all over the state for academic, sports, and military achievements, all in the name of Boys' High.

We learned a lot of lessons. Originally we planned our get-togethers for Friday nights, so we would not impinge on weekend activities and so people coming from afar (some from California and several from out of the country) would have at least the entire weekend in Atlanta. One of our members complained about Friday night, saying our Jewish members (who were many) had religious activities that night. We changed to Thursday, and wouldn't you know it—the complainer showed up early, sought me out, and said he appreciated the change but on this particular Thursday he would have to skip for business reasons.

Tom and Margaret Norman, along with their daughter Vicki, aided by Bill Rhodes, '44, Joe Lipsius, '36, and others, managed to compile a list of over 7,400 names of Boys' High graduates from the first class in 1872 to the last class of 1947. With something like 3,500 active addresses, Tom has engineered the publication of numerous directories over the years. At each meeting of the board of directors, the V.P. for Records reads the names of those who have gone "on to victory" since his last report. We're getting fewer.

Starting with the 1998 meeting, the board of directors decided to honor certain living members for outstanding contributions to Atlanta and to the nation.

First, of course, was Dean Rusk, celebrated as a scholar, teacher, soldier, diplomat and dispenser of philanthropy—"a creator of foreign policy, champion of world peace and wise tutor to succeeding generations."

We've also recognized:

Ivan Allen, Jr., '29, businessman, twice mayor of Atlanta, a giant in civic affairs and champion for civil rights in 1963.

Henry King Stanford, '33, distinguished educator, president of five colleges or universities, including the University of Georgia.

A.B. Padgett, '31, a humanitarian who, as V.P. for community affairs at the Trust Company Bank, provided financial assistance and leadership to many Atlanta Organizations.

Harlee Branch, Jr., '23, President of Georgia Power Company, then President and Chairman of the Board of Southern Company, and an international figure in the electric utilities field.

Henry L. Bowden, '28, Chairman of the Board of Trustees of Emory University, with valuable contributions to leading the University through racial desegregation.

Boisfeuillet Jones, '30, a teacher and administrator at Emory University, responsible for major strides toward excellence in Emory's medical center and later, as Chairman of Economic Opportunity Atlanta and the Georgia State Board of Human Resources, and President of the Emily and Ernest Woodruff Foundation, strengthened cooperation between those foundations and the practice of matching fund-raising by benefiting institutions.

And . . . many more whose names you will recognize in succeeding years:

Banker and philanthropist J. Mack Robinson;

Attorney, community leader and soldier Elliott Goldstein;

Attorney and member of Congress Robert G. Stephens;

Attorney and community servant Thomas Hal Clarke;

Teacher, administrator, and Legislator Ben F. Johnson, Jr.;

Architect, civic leader, combat aviator, and defender of human values Cecil Alexander;

Civic leader and Pulitzer Prize winner George E. Goodwin;

Business, military and civic leader Bernie Abrams;

Detroit Tigers' distinguished announcer Ernie Harwell;

President of the American Medical Association Dr. Harrison "Jack" Rogers.

One activity of the Association from the very start has been the publication of a newsletter, generally tri-annually. Sent to all identified living graduates, it garners much mail, both amusing and informative.

A letter from an old grad told us of an unusual activity during his term at BHS. Information about an activity called Screw Day spread covertly through the student body. The idea was that on one particular day every boy was to surreptitiously remove one screw from someplace in the building and drop it in a container in Ma Crawford's cafeteria. (Remember that all the schoolrooms had hinged-top wooden desks that were screwed down to the floor. Lotsa screws there. But there were also other screws.)

As the report went, when one teacher started to leave his room that afternoon the door came off in his hand! Supposedly two janitors spent a whole night getting everything reassembled.

A 1947 photo appeared in the October 1991 issue of the *Boys' High Alumni Association News* that showed the small gravel parking lot beside a partially dismantled "portable." In the background you can see the brick three-story main Henry Grady High School. In the foreground stand two pot-bellied stoves. Some months after that publication, one boy (possibly less perceptive but more nostalgic) queried the editor, "Do you know where I could find one of them?"

Only about forty-five years too late!

Another letter addressed itself to the oft-quoted statement that "A Boys' High School diploma gave an automatic entry to any university." The writer of that letter, a Harvard graduate, told us that he was admitted to Harvard on that premise. Midway through his freshman year, he was not doing so well and was called to the dean's office and asked, "How did you ever get in here?"

At one point in the late '30s, just before the annual Boys' High–Tech High football game, some Tech High boys managed to hoist a school flag made from sheet metal on the flagpole in front of the school. They then cut the halyards and greased the pole to prevent the flag's removal. A Ford convertible sedan, with fabric top up and buttoned-on isinglass windows installed, appeared in the Boys' High parking lot. A shotgun slid through the side window and blasted away at the flag, and the car sped away. That bullet-riddled metal flag became the property of Jim DeBardelaben, '39 (now a retired airline captain). He has donated it to the History Center where it resides in the Boys' High collection.

One boy wrote about the origin of our fight song, "On to Victory," recounting a time our distinguished football coach, R.L. "Shorty" Doyal was in the office of our principal, H.O. Smith. Outside the building the Tech High band was playing "On Wisconsin" and Doyal mentioned to Smith that the school should have a fight song. At that moment, a teacher (maybe it was our orchestra teacher, Gaines W. Walter) opened a notebook and dashed off the dear-to-all-the-old-grads words of "On to Victory" to the tune of "On Wisconsin."

Though the membership has dwindled, the scholarship fund has grown through the generosity of many, and the fund will continue to grow when the contributors are all gone. Many years in the future, a deserving student may receive an award and ask, "What was Boys' High School?" Though none of us will be around, our slogan, "Boys' High Forever!" will have come true.

What Happened

After being fifty-three years in the same location and serving millions from all over the world, Herren's finally closed its doors on Friday, November 13, 1987. During its last two or three years, it began to dawn on me that the end was approaching. But like the old fashioned, gutsy entrepreneur I thought I was, I keep telling myself, *"It's gonna get better."* It did . . . some. And it didn't . . . mostly.

My great brother-in-law, Chuck Satterthwaite (Rose's husband), once told me a story about a restaurant he worked for in Philadelphia or New York, part of a prominent chain of its day. Back in the '50s his unit was doing an annual business of something like three million dollars. One day, his bosses were discussing the difficulty of achieving the desired level of profit, a constant management subject in our business. "We'd be okay if we could only increase our gross business by a million dollars a year," the boss said. What a dream! That would produce a hefty increase in the bottom line for almost any small business. A whole lot less would have bailed us out.

I remember talking with an attorney friend whose firm represented, among their many corporate clients, a theater chain of some 700 units, as I remember it. The owner of that chain was an occasional guest and always showed all the signs of prosperity. I commented to my attorney friend, "If he personally made ten bucks each day from each of his theaters he'd be making a pile." The attorney sagely observed, "But what if he's losing that from each location each day?"

You never know.

I'm sure some of my guests, as well, maybe, as some of my lifelong friends and acquaintances, thought I closed Herren's because I was loaded with so much money I didn't want or need any more.

We didn't go bankrupt. (We couldn't afford a lawyer for that!) Besides, if I remember correctly, you can't bankrupt against taxes and rent, both of which figured largely in our accounts payable. We had simply become insolvent—unable to pay our bills.

Our landlord had, for about a year, been in court where he had been arguing with the heirs of the former owner of the building. The bone of contention was our rent, which was the only money being derived from the property. While they argued, each demanded rent from us and neither was willing to indemnify us in case the other side won the suit. In such case, we might have paid rent to one but ended up owing the other, with no recourse to the one who had collected. As you read on you will become aware that the cash flow was growing smaller every day. We declined to pay both of them.

What cash was developed was used to pay for food, supplies, and payroll. Our suppliers had put us on a C.O.D. basis when we closed the dinner business. We paid salaries (not mine . . . gone since three years earlier) and what other bills we could. But we got further behind on all our open accounts. Caught between a rock and a hard place we (Jane and I) regularly put thousands of our personal savings into the business until we were all but paupers ourselves.

Finally, in late summer of 1987, the tug of war between the two "landlords" was adjudicated, and the winner demanded all his back unpaid rent, ending in a court order that we pay within a few days (was it three or five?) or vacate. We managed a small reprieve by paying a portion of the missing rent and delayed the closing for a few days while we made arrangements to liquidate our paltry assets.

We closed after lunch on Friday the 13th, always a significant day in our family. Over that weekend we called every employee and scheduled a meeting for 10:00 A.M. on Monday the 18th. At that time I tearfully informed our great staff of our demise, and found most of them expected it. My chef (my newest "young man" and the only employee who knew) had spent that weekend in the building with me, inventorying the perishable food and assembling it in grocery bags to give a share to each employee, along with their final paycheck.

At the same time, on Saturday the 14th, the auction company we had hurriedly selected ran an ad stating that all our assets would be auctioned off on Saturday the 21st. The news staff of *The Atlanta Constitution* noticed the ad when it was placed on Friday and immediately sent a reporter. The sad story ran on Saturday the 14th along with our sweet roll recipe, which we had shared with their readers on numerous occasions.

As can be imagined, the auction day was one of great hope— that enough money would be generated to pay our bills—and one of great sadness, seeing the rape of our life's work. Amid this activity, there were moments of both promise and despair. Among the first things auctioned were our bar chairs—wooden captain's chairs, that brought about ten dollars apiece more than we had paid for them several years before. Our art collection, on the other hand, brought a pittance of its appraised value. One of our antique sideboards brought about $400 (I had years ago turned down an offer for $4,000). I still have an inventory somewhere showing the sales price of each item, but I've never studied it. The ultimate result was far below what was needed.

With the proceeds of the auction we were forced to pay our secured creditors, as far as the money would stretch. After that, the secured creditors had to be paid by Beautiful (but tearful) Jane and me, from what was left of our crumbled retirement pot. The dreams of retiring by selling the business to someone had been with me for a long time. What had happened?

Many years before, a young general manager had been hired with the understanding between us that he would ultimately be able to buy the business and would have had the experience to continue its operation. The idea was that he would, in effect, become my heir, since our three kids were not interested and were all involved in other activities.

I doodled lots of scenarios that would have put him in the ownership spot with me taking lots of paper from someone I loved and trusted who would honor our buy-out agreement. He would buy, using part of my salary for his payments. Maybe he could retain me as a part-time consultant like the big boys do. We went as far as to try to buy out my two brothers and sister, who still owned their 10% shares of the business. Understandably, he didn't want to buy the business and end up with the minority stockholders, whom he had never met, as his partners.

Two of the three agreed, but while all the negotiating was going on, time passed and other things were happening. We were struggling along with no or low profits, while still doing annual business over the million dollar mark. Neither of us was making a stellar salary, but we were keeping the business going. Meanwhile, our landlord had sold the building to an out-of-town developer who had assembled almost the entire block and was restoring the buildings as historic landmarks. It was a great idea but somewhere along the line he ran out of steam and money. In the early '80s he offered us the two small vacant spaces next door to build a bar, which we had never been able to fit into our peculiarly shaped space and the politics of the time.

It was the answer to a longtime dream, but, much as we liked the idea, we couldn't round up the needed cash. He said that if we didn't take it he would rent it to someone else for a bar and had a tenant in sight. Of course, if this was true, we couldn't have that. So Beautiful Jane and I borrowed as much as we could and cashed in what we could, and with lots of personal sweat by young man manager and me, we set out to build our bar. The two of us did just about all the demolition work ourselves and a significant part of the rebuilding. I drew all the plans for the bar (including the plan for the reflected ceiling) and ended up personally painting and papering the whole place.

While I was painting one day I became aware of a stranger who was watching me work. I thought that he might be from the union, but then he introduced himself. He owned a store nearby and offered me a job painting his store. Thank you, God, for giving me a good sense of humor.

On December 7, 1984, we added "Guido's . . . the place next door," named for my father. It had its own outside entrance on Luckie Street, and we had managed to carve out an entrance from Herren's lobby where the lobster tank used to reside. (The tank had been moved a few feet away.) Guido's also had an entrance into Herren's back dining room.

Guido's had a rectangular bar like the one on the TV show "Cheers" with seating at the bar and at tables around it in the rest of the space. The city's building code required that the space behind the bar, including the hinged-top entry, had to be wheelchair accessible, with room behind the bar for said wheelchair to be turned around. This we accomplished by building a removable cabinet under the cash register. But there was no requirement about bar height! In both back corners of the barroom we had cozy alcoves with round tables for five or more. One was regularly occupied in the late afternoon by some illustrious newspaper people, a group whose makeup varied from day to day.

Guido's had its own staff that served food from its own menu from Herren's kitchen. The smaller menu was more limited than the one next door but contained many familiar items plus some barroom specialties like nachos and buffalo wings. We tried to introduce curly fried potatoes because I thought they were great. I was the only one.

The menu had pictures of Guido's family from the old days, back to his time on the USS George Washington. The narrative on the menu told its readers his story and mentioned he would be surprised to see buffalo wings on his menu, since he didn't even know they had wings! The walls displayed pictures of old Atlanta, including a huge aerial view of our downtown taken from a spot approximately over the Georgia Tech campus. If you knew where to look, our building was right in the middle! Also displayed were some of Guido's mementos, including a newspaper column he had written for *The Atlanta Constitution* commenting on the quality of meat in the days of Genghis Khan and how it was tenderized (not printable here, or anywhere else, for that matter), and a copy on hardboard of the front of a piece of sheet music, his song "Rosita" that he wrote for my sister.

Over the years we had seen many buildings razed and replaced by some of the monoliths you now see in downtown Atlanta. Many were simply replaced by parking lots, pending someone's decision to build. Some properties simply became vacant. Downtown Atlanta was gradually dying, even though we had the appearance of progress. Down the street from us was a skeleton, the remnants of the old Georgia Hotel, stripped down to its steel bones and trash-strewn concrete floors. It stood there for many years while various developers unsuccessfully attempted its redevelopment. It was even used once as the set for a movie. (Its director John Huston, stars, and others lunched daily at Herren's for many days.)

When "Light Up Atlanta" was proposed in early 1984 by a

developer's public relations department, it sounded like an excellent idea. After a series of somber headlines and much word-of-mouth in the suburbs, Atlantans had become leery of downtown. The idea was to invite all those folks downtown for a gigantic street party to see how their town had grown and how great it was.

Along with most downtown businesses, I enthusiastically endorsed the plan and feverishly worked on implementing it. My young manager was put in charge of the restaurant group (in truth, the restaurants and bars were the mainstay of the event) and spent many hours working on the undertaking. Using our in-house walking map of downtown and printing facilities at Coca-Cola, he developed an outstanding publicity piece showing all the promotions of each individual enterprise. Each offered inducements to bring their hoped-for share of the expected crowd. The promoters let Atlantans know, via the Atlanta newspapers, what was about to happen.

We all chipped in to pay for the ads, with the developer taking the big end of the stick. Anyone who thinks that newspaper advertising, correctly used, doesn't work should have seen the turnout. On the selected night, the streets of the central area were closed to traffic and we had a gigantic street party with music, dancing in the streets, strolling singers, jugglers, mimes, and other outdoor activities, topped off by the lighting up of Atlanta. At the specified time, the mayor appeared in Central City Park (now called Woodruff Park, for its donor) to throw the switch that turned on all the lights in surrounding buildings. A great show!

Shade tree entrepreneurs showed up on the edges of this revelry with station wagons and trucks packed with cold beer, which they sold to all comers. The crowd became boisterous and the city was littered with empty cans. The merchants who promoted the whole thing were left holding the bag. The bars and restaurants remained empty while the revelers wandered the streets.

We had learned a lesson . . . we thought.

What we should have learned was that the majority of the crowd, the good people of Atlanta, were no match for the irresponsible people who attend such gatherings, people who didn't care about the city and weren't interested in anything or anyone except themselves. We saw the reckless few destroying the city, so lovingly and carefully built over so many years by the many.

When the same promotion was proposed for the next year, the city recognized some of the faults and, for a small fee, issued temporary permits to all who held valid liquor licenses. The permit entitled each holder to construct two temporary outdoor bars at designated spots for dispensing draft beer in disposable cups. If the event was operated by responsible people, it was assumed that the sobriety of the occasion might be improved. The health department monitored the design so that all the activities were behind screens, and running water had to be available for the bartenders to wash their hands. We continued the same promotions we had the previous year: some offered free wine with meals; others offered discounts, two-for-one deals, free dessert, and other similar enticements.

When the big night arrived, we experienced the same lack of interest in our dining rooms but did really well in the outdoor bars. But things got rowdy elsewhere. The bolder roughnecks invaded the Hyatt Regency Hotel, advancing to the upper floors where they threw furniture over the balcony rails of the atrium into the lobby many floors below. Luckily, no one was killed, but the roof of the Parasol Bar, a huge stained-glass parasol, was destroyed.

When the third year came around, the mayor refused to give a permit. Period.

Year four, 1986, I was unaware of the event until about a week before it was to happen. I don't believe any of my fellow restaurateurs were invited to participate, either. The event went off as scheduled with the crowd estimated to be two or three hundred thousand.

Atlantans will remember the Sunday and Monday headlines about crime in the streets, including maps of downtown with crime spots marked. Pickpockets, purse snatchers, and muggers were busy!

The "man" pointed a pistol at a policeman in the Five Points MARTA station and was shot.

Downtown crime made headlines. Years earlier a young employee of former Governor Carl Sanders had just emerged from a food shop across the street from her office in the Candler Building, about a block from Herren's, when she was accosted by a new-to-Atlanta deranged man who put a pistol to her head and pulled the trigger. He took two steps, put the gun to his own head and shot himself. The blood stains remained on the sidewalk for days afterward.

Likewise, a doctor attending an AMA convention was killed on the street. As I heard the story from a police friend, two couples left a restaurant about a mile from the center of the city, at the northernmost edge of the Central Business District, at about 1:00 A.M.; one was carrying a fancy wine bottle. They decided to walk the mile back to their hotel down Piedmont Avenue, a street that no Atlantan ever walked after dark, and encountered young punks who demanded their money. The doctor who was carrying the wine bottle tried to swing it at the culprits and was killed. New York newspapers called Atlanta "the crime capitol of the world."

Atlantans were still getting over these past events and many suburbanites who had not been to town in years were convinced it was still happening, as were people all over the world.

Light Up Atlanta '86 was the final blow. Within a week we closed at dinner for lack of business. There were more of us than there were of them. The first night we closed, I stayed by the front door with the telephone within reach to monitor our potential business. We would have had *six* guests that night. I thought that this might last a few weeks and then we could announce our re-opening.

After all, we were still honoring all the two-fers and our own $10.00 cash discount coupons. I felt that after a week or two people would start calling again for reservations. It never happened. Even the guests from the downtown hotels stopped coming.

Apparently, hotel workers were advising their guests not to go out or, if necessary, to take a cab. The mayor asked all the downtown business operators to meet with one of his department heads. Nearly everyone felt Light Up Atlanta had been a bummer with one or two exceptions. One bar owner whose business was at the very center of modern Atlanta (about four blocks from us) and also the center of all the "festivities" said his business had been only moderately good and added, as an aside to me down at the end of the table, "Ed, I've been in downtown Atlanta for many years, but I wouldn't walk down to your place at night anymore."

By this time my bright young man had gone on to a bigger and better world, possibly having realized that I was whistling in the dark. Another young man had come and gone. I was alone, operating a business that was serving five lunches each week, hoping to hang on until things got better. Our books showed lunch business to be $64,000 to $70,000 per month, and it was worth a try to see if expenses could be pared to stay alive at that point for a few months. But by the time the end came in November, a year later, we were down to about $38,000 per month. Those left in the offices around us scrambled to make arrangements to move and did so in the ensuing months.

Today our old neighborhood stands almost totally deserted. The Rialto Theater closed shortly after we did and now, five years later at this writing, has finally been taken over by the Performing Arts Center for Georgia State University.

Most of the other buildings in the block have been taken over by the University, the gift of a local philanthropist and others. Our most recent landlord declared bankruptcy even before we left, and the building was ultimately bought by the present owner, who is converting it into a home for Theatrical Outfit, Atlanta's second oldest theatre company.

R.I.P.

requiescat in pace
which in Southern means,
"No More Sweet Rolls."

EPILOGUE

The story of Herren's is a continuing saga and you may wish to hear more.

In the ensuing years, someone unknown to me bought the building out of bankruptcy, but it remained empty. For a short period it was occupied by a construction company, building something on a nearby vacant lot . . . then boarded up again with a "For Sale" sign. In 1993, Jane and I moved to Ellijay, in the beautiful mountains of North Georgia, and rarely visited Atlanta.

In early 2003 I received a call from Mike Cain, a friend from the Village Writers Group in Atlanta. He told me that a friend of his had bought the Herren's building and found out from Mike that I was still kicking. He wanted to meet me, so the next morning Jane and I met Mike, who introduced us to Bill Balzer, a retired UPS executive and buyer of the Herren's building! They took us to lunch at a local restaurant and we got to know Bill.

We had already seen a front page newspaper article showing Tom Key, Producer and Artistic Director of Theatrical Outfit, standing in front of Herren's and stating that the building was to become the home of the theatrical group. Bill and his wife Peg had bought the building and planned on donating it.

A short time later Bill brought Peg to Ellijay and we had a most enjoyable visit as they pored over the contents of several banana boxes of Herren's memorabilia. They borrowed many of our old photos, menus and other pieces which they later returned when they brought Bill's mother up to see the North Georgia mountains. Some of the pictures now appear in the theater's promotion booklet. It seems that Herren's will be reborn, this time as a theater and a new star in downtown Atlanta. And Bill has assured me that they'll be serving Herren's sweet rolls!

INDEX